HISTORIC MODELS
of Early America

HISTORIC MODELS

of Early America

AND HOW TO MAKE THEM

by C. J. MAGINLEY

ILLUSTRATED WITH NUMEROUS DIAGRAMS
BY JAMES MACDONALD

HARCOURT, BRACE & WORLD, INC.
NEW YORK

TO RUTH

I wish to express my sincere appreciation to Miss Elisabeth D. McKee for her invaluable assistance in preparing the working drawings for this book.

CONTENTS

FOREWORD   xi

INTRODUCTION   xiii

    TOOLS   xiii
    MATERIALS—WOOD   xiv
    MATERIALS—MISCELLANEOUS   xiv
    FINISHING THE MODELS   xv
    GENERAL SUGGESTIONS   xv
    MAKING WHEELS   xvi
    OX YOKE   xviii
    WHIPPLE TREES   xix
    NECK YOKE   xix
    DIAGRAMS FOR HORSE AND OX   xx

TRANSPORTATION IN EARLY AMERICA

    A VIKING SHIP   3
    A TRAVOIS   8
    A LOG CANOE OR PIROGUE   10
    AN OX CART   12
    A TOBACCO ROLLER   16
    AN EARLY SLEIGH   19
    THE ONE-HORSE SHAY   23
    THE CONESTOGA WAGON   28
    THE CONCORD COACH   34
    A RIVER FLATBOAT   46
    THE CLERMONT   49
    A CANAL PACKET   55
    A HORSE CAR   60

CONTENTS

THE TOM THUMB   66
THE MERRIMAC   75
THE MONITOR   79
AN EARLY BICYCLE——THE ORDINARY   82
THE FIRST FORD   87
THE FIRST AIRPLANE   95

ON EARLY AMERICAN FARMS

AN EARLY PLOW   103
A WOODEN HARROW   107
A GRAIN CRADLE   110
A FLAIL   113
A SAMP MILL   115
A WATER WHEEL AND GRIST MILL   117

IN EARLY AMERICAN HOMES

A CRADLE   123
A HORNBOOK   126
A FOOT STOVE   128
A SETTLE   131
A BUTTER CHURN   134
A WOOL WHEEL   137

IN EARLY AMERICAN VILLAGES

A LOG CABIN   141
A WELL SWEEP   145
THE STOCKS   148
THE PILLORY   150
THE DUCKING STOOL   153

FOREWORD

THE THINGS people use in their daily lives tell what those people are like, what they do, how they do it, the quality of their thinking and of their accomplishment. A careful study of a man's belongings, his clothes, his house, his tools, his books, his toys, will tell you all you need to know about him.

Here are pictured the things our forefathers used and in them is the essence of our history. The spinning wheel speaks eloquently of the need for clothing and the way the women met it. The hornbook tells of the colonists' love of learning and of their determination to secure it for their children. Here is the plow, a primitive tool, which made the difference between starvation and food, life and death. And the grain cradle speaking of the slow careful work that prepared the grain for the kitchen and the barns. Study the water wheel that ground the corn between its ponderous, rumbling stones, and contrast it with the great mills of today—so efficient, so swift, so huge—grinding the wheat that feeds the nations. The long road we have traveled since these things were used has been built by the strength and skill of men's hands.

This book is the basis for an understanding of our country's history. Children will enjoy it and through it they can handle, study and make the things their forefathers made and used.

Learning dates and lists of battles is not the way to learn history. Let children begin their study of history in their own neighborhood, visit the old historic sites, study the old maps, talk to the old people, and then build a model of their home place with the houses and the things people used. Such a way of learning is a way of sharing the rich experiences that nourish each generation and stimulate the growth of the next generation. In this thought lies the reason for this book.

ANGELO PATRI

INTRODUCTION

TOOLS

IN DESCRIBING the construction of all models it has been assumed that only hand tools will be available to the model builder. The tools with which all of the models can be made are:

Coping saw with fine blades
Keyhole saw
Small hand drill and assorted drills which should include numbers 43, 45, 52, 55, and 60 also a ⅛″ and ¼″ drill
Tack hammer
Small vise
Small files—flat, pointed, round
Emery boards
Small pliers
Sharp pointed knife
Try square
Compass
Awl
Small screw driver
Ruler
Pin vise
One-edge razor blades
Scissors
Side cutting pliers or reed cutters
Clamps
Chisel
Saw jack
Sandpaper 00, 0, 1

INTRODUCTION

If any power tools are to be purchased a magnetic jig saw will be of greatest use for cutting out the parts. These saws can be purchased for between five and ten dollars.

MATERIALS—WOOD

California pine, also known as sugar pine, is an excellent wood for model making. Other soft woods which are good are white pine and bass wood. Maple is a very good hard wood to use. These can be obtained from a woodworking shop or a lumber dealer who will saw them to the required thickness.

Aircraft plywood, which can be purchased at the hobby store in different thicknesses, is another excellent wood for models. This material does not split easily and the thinner pieces can be cut with a sharp knife or razor blade.

Balsa wood can be purchased in almost any size needed for the models and is very easy to work with. It is graded according to the degree of hardness and it is advisable to purchase the hardest grade.

Many good pieces of wood can be obtained from the scrap pile in any woodworking or cabinet maker's shop. Fruit boxes, cheese boxes, cigar boxes and berry baskets contain much wood that can be used.

Other sources of wood are pot or plant labels, which can be purchased at the hardware store, and medicine applicators at the drugstore. Spools, checkers, buttonmolds, dowels, toothpicks, matches and beads may also be used.

MATERIALS—MISCELLANEOUS

Cement
Glue
Plastic wood
Common pins
Veil and corsage pins
Paper clips

14, 18, 20 gauge copper wire
Reed no. 1, 2
Copper foil
Tin
Cellophane
Thin leather
Rubber bands
Plastic straws
Pencils
Corncob pipestems
Broomstraws
Wheels from old clocks

FINISHING THE MODELS

The models may be finished by applying an oil stain. If the stain is too dark it can be diluted with linseed oil. A maple stain is very effective for many of the models. Or, if you prefer the natural wood finish, use a clear lacquer.

GENERAL SUGGESTIONS

Throughout the book, *pc* stands for *piece.*

Use wood always unless another material is specifically mentioned.

Use the try square to make sure the edge of the wood is square and for drawing lines on wood.

Always sandpaper the wood until it is smooth. The difference between a good model and a poor one may depend on how well it is sandpapered.

Sandpaper small pieces by rubbing them on a large piece of sandpaper laid on the workbench.

When tracing patterns use a ruler to draw the straight lines.

When making two pieces just alike, such as the sides for a carriage, put them in the vise and sandpaper both pieces until they are exactly the same shape and size.

INTRODUCTION

Pound wire with a hammer to flatten it for braces, steps and the like. By pounding the wire on an old file very realistic steps can be made. Be sure to use an old file as you may break it.

Put one end of a piece of wire in the vise and pull it with the pliers to make it straight.

Flat toothpicks make excellent pegs. Do not use nails in making the models. Use pegs, cement, glue, and common pins or escutcheon pins.

When working a piece of wood until it is round, keep turning it as you file or sandpaper it. Also, when sawing off a piece of round stick turn it between the partly opened jaws of the vise as you saw, or if using a knife or razor blade turn the piece on the workbench.

Before sawing along a line with the coping saw, make a cut part way through the wood with a knife. It will then be easier to follow the line with the saw.

MAKING WHEELS

Many of the models described in this book require wheels. While wooden discs are used on a few models most of them will need wheels with spokes. Wood $\frac{3}{16}''$ thick is used for most of the rims although $\frac{1}{8}''$ wood may be used for some of the lighter wheels. Either hard wood or soft wood can be used for the rims. Maple is a good hard wood to use, but soft woods cut more easily. Aircraft plywood is excellent for the rims. The spokes can be made from reed, applicators, broomstraws, balsa strips or toothpicks.

Three methods of constructing wheels will be described but whichever method is used the first step is to draw a circle with a compass. Draw another circle about $\frac{3}{16}''$ inside the outer one. Then, before cutting the disc out, use the try square to draw two diameters perpendicular to each other. These lines will make it easier to space the spokes. Cut out the disc and smooth off the edges before sawing out the inner circle.

Method 1. Make a groove around the hub, about ³⁄₃₂″ deep and equidistant from the ends, with a file which is about ¹⁄₁₆″ thick. Make a saw cut first and then enlarge with the file. It is easier to cut the grooves before cutting off the hub to the correct length. Lay the piece in the partly opened jaws of the vise and turn with one hand while filing or sawing. In this way the groove will be cut straight around the piece. Drill a hole lengthwise through the center of the hub for the axle. Drill another hole, the size of the spokes being used, through the hub in the opposite direction. This hole should go through the hub where the groove was made. Taper one end of the hub.

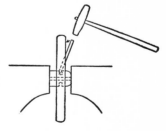

Cut a piece of material, from which the spokes are to be made, the length of the inside diameter of the rim. Put this piece through the hole drilled crosswise in the hub and set it and the hub inside of the rim with the hub in the center of the rim. Then cut off the spokes just a trifle longer than the distance between the bottom of the groove and the inside of the rim. Flatten one end of each spoke a little by pinching it in the vise or with pliers so that it will fit snugly into the groove. Put the hub and rim into the vise. Tap one end of the spoke into the hub groove and press the rim over the other end. If the spoke is too long take it out and rub the end on sandpaper. After the length of the spokes has been determined put some glue in the groove and on the outer end of each spoke as it is set in place. When the wheel is finished redrill the hole through the hub for the axle.

Method 2. Divide the circle into 8, 12, or 16 equal parts depending on the number of spokes to be put in and saw out the disc. At the outer end of each radius make a mark on the circumference. With an awl make a small hole in the exact center of the circumference at each mark and drill

a hole to a depth of about ⅜″ into the disc. The size of the hole will depend upon the size of the spoke used. Then proceed as explained in Method 1, only insert the spokes through the holes in the rim and into the groove made in the hub.

Method 3. Draw a ½″ circle at the center of the disc for the hub. Draw four diameters at equal distances apart. Then draw a line ¹⁄₁₆″ from each side of the diameters and parallel to them to indicate the edges of the spokes. Cut out the wood between the spokes and round off their edges with an emery board or small file.

Flanged wheels for the locomotive models can be made by making a saw cut around the circumference of the disc before the inner circle is cut out. Then with a knife and file remove the wood to a depth of about ¹⁄₁₆″ on one side of the cut.

Another way to make a flanged wheel is to cut a disc from ¹⁄₁₆″ wood with a diameter ⅛″ longer than the diameter of the other disc. Glue the two discs together and then saw out the inside leaving a rim with a flange.

OX YOKE

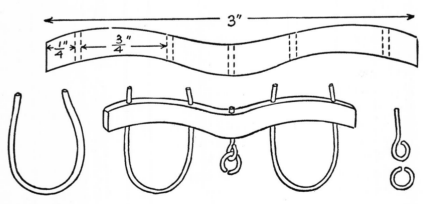

Materials:

1 pc ³⁄₁₆″ x ½″ x 3″—bar
2 pc no. 2 reed or broomstraws 3″ long—bows

1 pc 18 gauge wire ⅝″ long—bolt
1 pc 18 gauge wire ¾″ long—ring

Trace the pattern for the bar. Drill the holes just large enough for the bows and drill a pin hole for the bolt. Bend the bows and insert in the holes. Make the bolt and ring.

WHIPPLE TREES

Materials:

1 pc ⅛″ x ⅜″ x 3″—double tree
2 pc ⅛″ dowel 2″ long—single trees
6 pc 20 gauge wire ½″ long
2 pc 20 gauge wire ⅜″ long

Shape the double tree and drill pin holes as indicated. Drill pin holes in the center of each end of the single trees about ¼″ in depth, and also through the single tree equidistant from the ends. Taper each end. Bend the wire parts to desired shape and assemble.

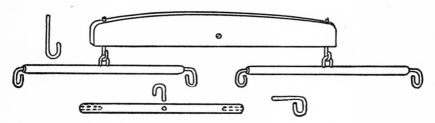

NECK YOKE

Materials:

1 pc ³⁄₁₆″ dowel 3″ long or 1 pc ³⁄₁₆″ x ³⁄₁₆″ x 3″
2 pc 18 gauge wire ¾″ long
1 pc 18 gauge wire 1″ long

Drill no. 60 holes ⅛″ in from each end and through the center. Make the metal parts for the ends by bending the wire around

a ⅛″ drill or dowel. Bend the wire for the center ring around
a ³⁄₁₆″ drill or dowel.

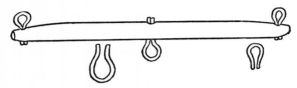

DIAGRAMS FOR HORSE AND OX

Trace the drawing, transfer outline to soft wood about ½″ in
thickness and saw out. Round off the edges with a file and sandpaper or work down to shape with a sharp knife. The ox or horse
may then be yolked to any appropriate model.

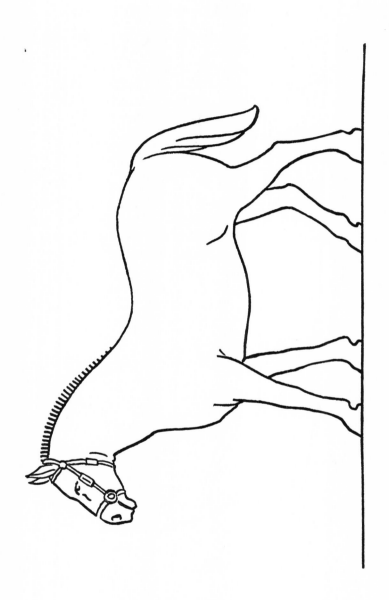

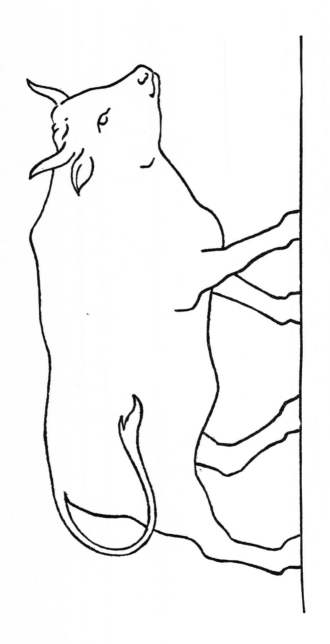

TRANSPORTATION IN EARLY AMERICA

A VIKING SHIP

MANY CENTURIES AGO the Norsemen or "Vikings" sailed out from their homes in northern Europe on voyages of adventure and plunder. They crossed the rough and stormy waters of the north Atlantic in open ships and sailed to other shores in search of riches and new lands. These ships, with the dragon's head at the prow, the brightly colored sail, and the warriors' shields hung along the sides, carried Leif Ericson and other hardy Norsemen to the shores of America as early as the ninth or tenth century, many years before Columbus discovered the New World.

Materials:

1 pc soft wood 1″ x 1″ x 6″—hull
1 pc ³⁄₁₆″ x 2″ x 7½″—for center piece
8 pc ¹⁄₃₂″ x ¼″ x 6½″—sheathing
1 pc ⅛″ dowel 5″ long—mast
1 pc applicator 3½″ long—yard
1 pc white paper 3½″ x 3″—sail
2 pc 20 gauge wire 3″ long
1 pc white paper 1¼″ x 2½″—canvas cover (roof)
20 ⅜″ buttonmolds, thumb tacks or upholstery tacks—shields
20 straight pins—shield hangers (if buttonmolds are used)
    Fine, dark green or black thread for stays and braces
2 pc ¹⁄₁₆″ x ⅝″ x 1″ ⎫
1 pc applicator 2¼″ long ⎬ stand
18 toothpicks—oars
1 pc ¹⁄₁₆″x ⅜″ x 1¾″—for steering oar

1. Draw a line *ab* lengthwise ¼″ in from one edge of the board from which the center piece is to be cut. Also draw lines *cd* and *ef*, 1½″ in from either end of the board. Trace the drawings for the prow and stern on tracing paper. Cut out these drawings and use them as patterns. Lay the end of the pattern for the prow on line *cd* and draw around it. Do the same for the stern by laying the end of the pattern so as to coincide with line *ef*. Saw around the outer edge of the center piece first. Before sawing around the inner line shape the head and tail with a file. Round off the edges.

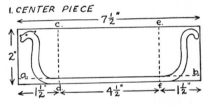

I. CENTER PIECE

4

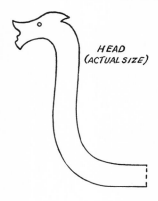

HEAD
(ACTUAL SIZE)

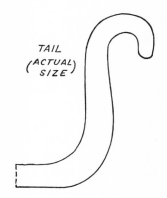

TAIL
(ACTUAL SIZE)

2. Trace hull pattern on piece of wood and shape it so as to fit inside the center piece. With a knife and chisel scoop out the wood inside the hull, leaving the decks at both ends as shown in the diagrams. Set the hull in the center piece and glue or peg in place.

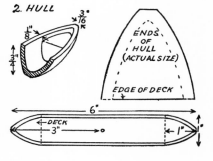

2. HULL

ENDS OF HULL (ACTUAL SIZE)

EDGE OF DECK

3. Start at the bottom of the model and sheathe with thin strips of wood. Overlap each strip and glue to the strip below it and to both ends of the center piece. Hold in place, until set, with rubber bands. Cut off the ends with a knife or razor blade. Instead of sheathing the ship, lines or grooves about ⅛" apart may be made with an awl lengthwise on the hull to represent planks.

3. SHEATHING HULL

5

4. Paint stripes on sail or use strips of colored Scotch tape. Make a ¼″ hem in each side of the sail. Lay a 3″ piece of wire in each hem and glue fast. When dry bend the sail around a tin can. This will make sail curve as though filled with wind. Lash the yard to the mast about ¾″ from the top. Fasten the sail to the yard by threading a needle and pulling needle and thread through the sail. Then tie thread in knot. Make an ⅛″ hole in the center of the roof piece. Fold in the center lengthwise and insert the lower end of the mast in this hole. Drill an ⅛″ hole in the center of the bottom of the hull and set the mast assembly into this hole. Tie the forestay and shrouds to the mast, the backstays to the yard, and the sheets to the lower corners of the sail. Fasten to the hull with small wire staples.

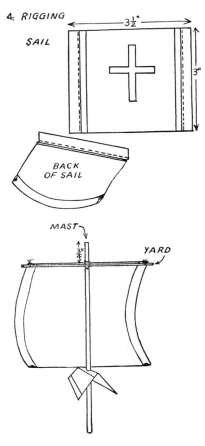

4. RIGGING

SAIL

3½″

3″

BACK OF SAIL

MAST

3¾″

YARD

5. Shape the oars from flat toothpicks. Make 9 no. 60 holes about
½″ apart along each side for the oars. Make the steering oar as
shown. Peg or glue it to the right side of the ship about 1″ from
the stern. If buttonmolds are used for the shields cement a pin in
each mold and bend it over to form a hook. Cut off the sharp end
of the pin so that it is about ½″ long. Make the standard as shown.
When making the holes for the brace, drill both pieces together
to insure getting the holes directly opposite each other. Paint or
dye the shields some bright color. Stain and shellac the model.
Use gilt paint for the serpent's head and tail.

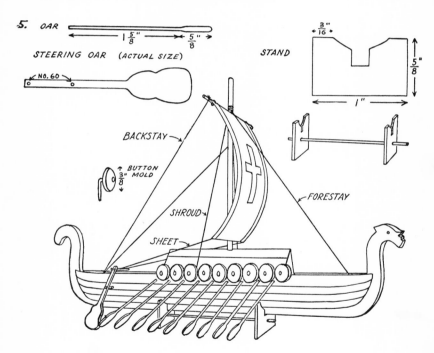

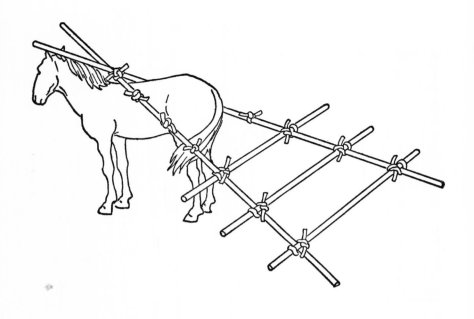

A   TRAVOIS

THE TRAVOIS, a pole frame dragged by a horse, was one of the earliest means of land transportation. It was used by the Indians of North America to carry their possessions when they moved from one camp to another, and was named travois by Frenchmen who explored the New World.

It was usually made by the Indian women and consisted of two poles crossed and fastened together at one end, with the other ends dragging on the ground, one on each side of the horse. Two or three crosspieces were tied to the poles near the ground, making a framework on which the household goods were carried. Young children, who were not able to walk, often sat on the top of the load and rode along behind the horse. Smaller travois were also made for dogs.

Materials:

2 pc applicator 6½″ long—poles
3 pc applicator 3¼″ long—crosspieces
   Some narrow strips of thin pliable leather cut from a chamois cloth or an old glove or mitten
   String or thread can be used if leather is not available

Cross two applicators at one end and bind together with a piece of leather about 1¼″ from the end. Cut 3 3¼″ pieces from the other two applicators.

Bind these pieces to the crossed pieces with the narrow leather thongs. Tie other pieces of the leather around the poles where they fit over horse's back.

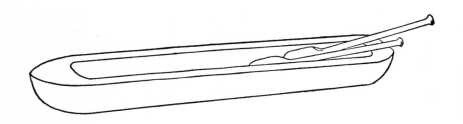

A LOG CANOE OR PIROGUE

THE EARLIEST FORM of boat used by the English colonists in America was like the log canoe used by the Indians. It was made from a tree trunk which was shaped and hollowed out with cutting tools and by fire. These crude, heavy boats were called pirogues by the colonists and were usually from fifteen to thirty feet in length and about three feet in diameter. These early boats were propelled through the water by means of short paddle-like oars.

Materials:

1 round stick about 1½″ in diameter and 8″ long (A piece cut from a tree branch or a bush makes a very realistic canoe. However, if this is not available the boat can be shaped from a piece of soft wood.)

2 pc ⅛″ x ⅜″ x 4″—paddles

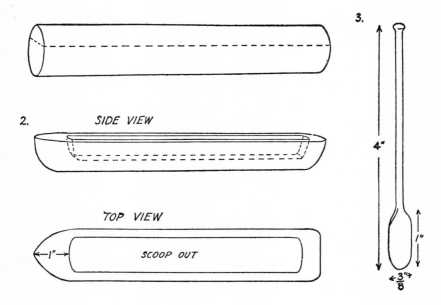

1. With a knife or saw cut away one side of the stick so as to make it flat. Cut off about ⅓ of the stick. Make one end come to a point. Round off the back end of the boat.

2. Draw outline of the part to be removed on the flat side of the stick. With a knife cut around this outline. Remove wood with a chisel to a depth of about ¾″. Smooth with sandpaper.

3. Draw the paddles on the pieces of wood. Cut out with a knife or saw. Shape with a file and sandpaper.
   Stain the boat and paddles.

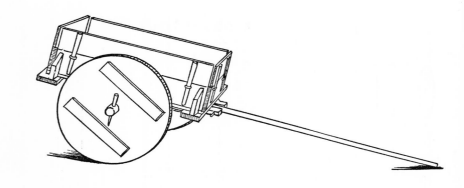

AN OX CART

IN COLONIAL AMERICA, oxen helped man in many ways. They hauled the stones from the fields, dragged the logs from the forest, drew the crude plow through the virgin soil and performed many other tasks for their owners.

The ox cart was a crude vehicle, with heavy wooden wheels sawed from a hardwood log, but it served its purpose and in the days when farm tools were scarce the man who owned an ox cart and a pair of sturdy oxen thought himself fortunate indeed.

Materials:

2 pc ⅛″ x ¾″ x 4″—side boards
2 pc ⅛″ x ¾″ x 2¾″—end boards
1 pc ¹⁄₁₆″ x 2¾″ x 4¼″—bottom of box
2 pc ⅛″ x ½″ x 3¼″—to reinforce box
4 pc ⅛″ x ¼″ x ¾″—braces for box
1 pc ³⁄₁₆″ x ⅝″ x 4¾″—axle
2 pc ⅛″ x 1¼″ x 2¾″—tongue supports or braces
1 pc ⅛″ x ¼″ x 1½″—crosspiece
1 pc ⅛″ dowel 6″ long—tongue
2 discs ³⁄₁₆″ thick and 2¾″ in diameter—wheels
4 pc ¹⁄₁₆″ x ¼″ x 2″—to reinforce wheels
2 pc ¹⁄₁₆″ x ⅝″ x 4⅛″—extra side boards
2 pc ¹⁄₁₆″ x ⅝″ x 2¾″—extra end boards
10 flat toothpicks
   20 gauge wire—staples and hooks

1. Drill a pinhole ½" in from each end and ⅛" down from the top of each of the side and end boards. Make the box by gluing the end boards to the side boards. Then glue on the bottom. Glue the two pieces used to reinforce the box in place. Allow the rear plank to extend ⅛" beyond the tail gate. The front plank should be even with the front end of the box. Both planks will extend ¼" beyond each side of the box at each end.

Shape the braces and glue them to the sides of the box ³⁄₁₆" in from one end. The lower ends of the braces will rest on the planks. Make 8 staples from wire and put the long end into each of the holes made in the ends and sides. Carefully press the other end of the staple into the wood with pliers. Glue 1¼" pieces of toothpicks to the extra end and side boards. The toothpicks on the side boards will be about 3" apart and about 1¾" apart on the end boards.

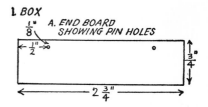

1. BOX

A. END BOARD
SHOWING PIN HOLES

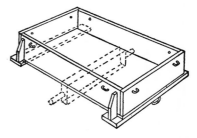

B. BOX ASSEMBLED

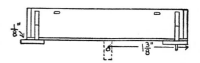

C. SIDE VIEW

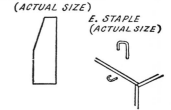

D. SIDE VIEW OF BRACE
(ACTUAL SIZE)

E. STAPLE
(ACTUAL SIZE)

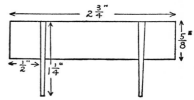

F. EXTRA END BOARD

2. Shape the axle and round off the ends. Drill no. 60 holes, ¼″ in from each end for pegs to hold the wheels on. Make two more staples and insert them into pinholes made in the axle 1½″ apart. Glue the axle to the box equidistant from the ends and with the staples toward the front.

3. Make the two tongue supports or braces as shown. Drill pinholes in the ends for wire hooks to fasten the tongue assembly to the axle. Drill a pinhole in the tongue ½″ back of the bolt, through the braces and tongue, for a wire hook which, with a wire staple in the plank beneath the front end of the box, will keep the cart from tipping backward.

Glue the pieces for strengthening the wheels to the wheels, in each of which an ⅛″ hole has been drilled for the axle. Put the wheels on the axle and insert pegs in the holes in the axle. Hook on the tongue assembly. Put the extra side boards in place. Make an ox yoke and a pair of oxen and the model is complete.

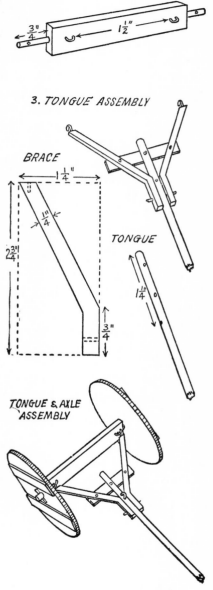

2. AXLE

3. TONGUE ASSEMBLY

BRACE

TONGUE

TONGUE & AXLE ASSEMBLY

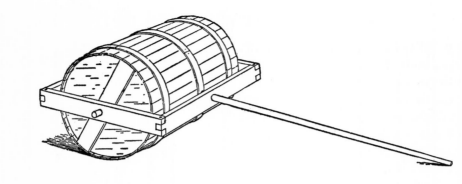

A TOBACCO ROLLER

THE ENGLISHMEN who settled in Virginia in the early seventeenth century found that they could become wealthy by raising tobacco. Acre upon acre of tobacco plants were put under cultivation in the rich Virginia soil.

When the leaves had been cured they were packed in huge casks ready for shipment to England. The easiest way to move the casks to the river warehouses was to roll them. The casks were pulled by men or drawn by horses or oxen to the river's edge where they were stored until they could be loaded onto ships. If the plantation was some distance from the warehouse, a box was often set in front of the cask to carry food for the horses or oxen and the driver.

A TOBACCO ROLLER

Materials:

2 discs $\frac{3}{16}''$ thick 2″ in diameter—ends of casks
28 pc $\frac{1}{16}''$ x $\frac{1}{4}''$ x 3″—sides of casks
2 pc $\frac{1}{8}''$ x $\frac{1}{4}''$ x 2″—end braces
2 pc $\frac{1}{8}''$ x $\frac{3}{8}''$ x 3″—ends ⎤
2 pc $\frac{1}{8}''$ x $\frac{3}{8}''$ x $3\frac{1}{2}''$—front and back ⎦ frame
1 pc $\frac{1}{8}''$ dowel $5\frac{1}{2}''$ long—tongue
2 pc $\frac{1}{8}''$ dowel 1″ long—axles
3 pc $\frac{1}{32}''$ x $\frac{1}{8}''$ x 8″—bands around cask

1. Drill an $\frac{1}{8}''$ hole in the center of each endpiece. Then make the cask by gluing the sidepieces to the two ends like a barrel. Allow each piece to overlap at each end by an $\frac{1}{8}''$. Drill an $\frac{1}{8}''$ hole in the center of each end brace. Glue one brace to each end of the cask so that the hole coincides with the hole in the end of the cask. Soak the thin strips and put them around the cask. Hold them in place with rubber bands until dry. Then glue the ends of the strips together.

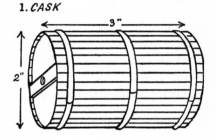

1. *CASK*

2. Cut the sections for the frame as shown. Make an ⅛″ hole in the center of the front piece for the tongue. Set the front and back pieces into the notches cut in the endpieces and glue or peg them fast. Shape the tongue and glue it in the hole in the front piece. Set the frame over the barrel and insert the axles through the holes in the frame and the holes in the barrel.

Saw out oxen or carve them from soft wood. Oxen should be about 4″ long and 2½″ in height. Make a yoke for the oxen.

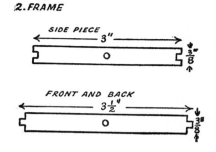

2. FRAME

SIDE PIECE

FRONT AND BACK

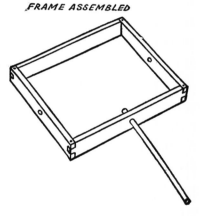

FRAME ASSEMBLED

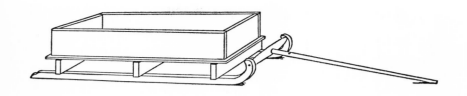

AN EARLY SLEIGH

IN EARLY COLONIAL DAYS, when there were few vehicles with wheels and the roads were little more than trails, people in the northern colonies did most of their traveling during the winter. Then the roads were made smooth and firm by a deep blanket of snow, and streams and rivers became solid highways of ice so that travel in sleighs was comparatively easy. It was then that the articles produced on the farm during the year were hauled to market and it was also the time for visits to the homes of friends, as there was less work to be done on the farms. There were many types of sleighs in use during the seventeenth and eighteenth centuries in America, and long caravans of them, loaded with farm produce, could be seen wending their way along the frozen highways of New England and the middle colonies on their way to the town or city. One common type was known as the Dutch sleigh. The people of New England called a sleigh drawn by two horses a pung and a one-horse sleigh a pod.

Materials:

2 pc $\frac{1}{16}$″ x 1″ x 6″—sides ⎤
2 pc $\frac{1}{8}$″ x 1″ x 2$\frac{1}{8}$″—ends ⎬ box
1 pc $\frac{1}{16}$″ x 2$\frac{1}{2}$″ x 6$\frac{1}{4}$″—bottom ⎦
3 pc $\frac{3}{16}$″ x $\frac{1}{2}$″ x 2$\frac{3}{4}$″—cross braces
2 pc $\frac{3}{16}$″ x 1″ x 7$\frac{1}{2}$″—for runners
1 pc $\frac{1}{4}$″ dowel 2$\frac{1}{8}$″ long—draw bar
1 pc $\frac{1}{8}$″ dowel 5$\frac{1}{2}$″ long—tongue
18 gauge wire for tongue brace

1. Trace pattern for runners on the wood and saw them out. Drill no. 60 holes in the curved end of each runner ¼″ down from the top. Peg or glue the three cross braces to the runners.

2. Make the box and glue it to the cross braces.

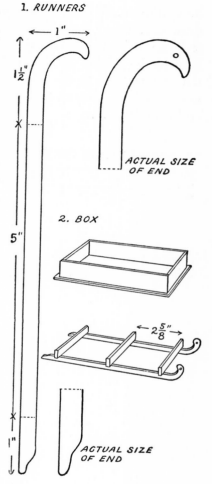

1. *RUNNERS*

2. *BOX*

3. Drill a no. 60 hole ¼″ in depth in the center of each end of the draw bar. Taper the tongue as shown in the diagram and insert it in an ⅛″ hole drilled through the draw bar. Drill a no. 60 hole in the tongue ¾″ from the rear end for the pin to fasten the double trees to the tongue. Fasten the draw bar and tongue assembly in place with toothpick pegs. Make a set of double trees and a neck yoke.

3. DRAWBAR AND TONGUE

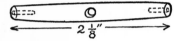

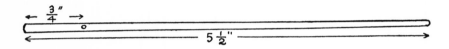

THE ONE-HORSE SHAY

OLIVER WENDELL HOLMES made one early American vehicle famous in his poem *The Deacon's Masterpiece* or, *The Wonderful One-Hoss Shay*. The American shay, more correctly known as the chaise, was a descendant of the two-wheeled French chaise and was well adapted for use on the dirt roads in this country a century and more ago. The American carriage builders improved upon the French vehicle and, with its leather thorough braces and large sturdy wheels, it was used in the United States as late as the time of the Civil War. The "One-Hoss Shay" was the forerunner of the buggy which replaced the shay as a passenger vehicle.

23

Materials:

2 pc plywood ¹⁄₁₆″ x 1″ x 3″—sides
1 pc plywood ¹⁄₁₆″ x 1″ x 2⅛″—back
1 pc plywood ¹⁄₁₆″ x 1¼″ x 2¼″—dash
1 pc ³⁄₁₆″ x 2⅛″ x 2¹³⁄₁₆″—floor
1 pc ³⁄₁₆″ x 1¾″ x 2⅛″—back ⎤
1 pc ³⁄₁₆″ x 1″ x 2⅛″—bottom ⎬ seat
2 pc ³⁄₁₆″ x ¾″ x 1″—supports ⎦
2 pc ⅛″ x ³⁄₁₆″ x 8¼″—shafts
2 pc ¹⁄₁₆″ x ⅛″ x 3½″—back crosspieces
1 pc ⅛″ x ⅛″ x 3⅛″—upper crosspiece
1 pc ⅛″ x ⅛″ x 3″—front crosspiece
2 pc ⅛″ x 1¾″ x 4″—body supports
2 pc 18 gauge wire 2″ long—steps
1 pc ³⁄₁₆″ x ¼″ x 4¾″—axle
2 16 spoke wheels 3½″ in diameter with hubs ⅜″ in diameter
   and ½″ long
2 pc thin leather ⅛″ wide and 7″ long—thorough braces
1 pc round toothpick 2″ long—single tree
   Covering for top—thin leather or cloth
3 pc 18 gauge wire 8″ long—top frame
2 pc 18 gauge wire 1¾″ long—stays

1. Trace pattern for sides on the wood and cut out. File off the back end of the floor board to make it slant a little like the sides. Glue on the back, then glue the sides to the floor and put on the dash.

2. Fasten the seat support to the sides about ¼″ in front of the backpiece. Glue on the seat bottom and the back which have been rounded off at the edges. Drill pinholes through each side and seat support ⅜″ from the front edge of the side and ¼″ down from the upper edge for the pins to hold the top braces.

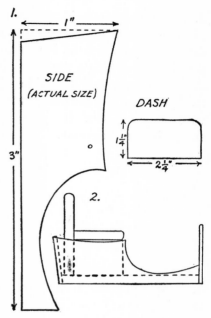

3. Make the loops in the ends of the top braces first. Then bend them to shape. Set the braces in position by putting a pin through the loops and into the side of the body. Connect the braces with wire stays. Cover the top as shown in the diagrams.

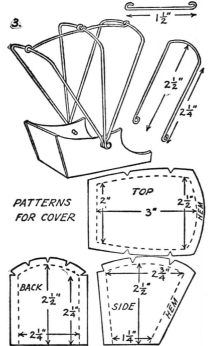

PATTERNS
FOR COVER

4. Sandpaper the front part of the shafts until they are round and about an ⅛″ in diameter. Bend the shafts to the approximate shape shown by holding over a flame or after soaking; or saw the shafts from a piece of wood ³⁄₁₆″ thick. Round off each end of the axle and glue the axle to the underside of the shafts 1⅜″ from the rear end.

Glue the two back crosspieces to the rear end of the shafts. Glue the front crosspiece to the shafts 4½″ back from the front end.

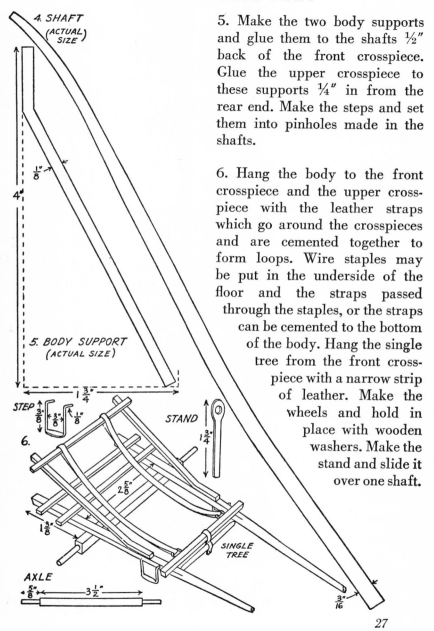

4. SHAFT (ACTUAL SIZE)

$\frac{1}{8}$″

4″

5. BODY SUPPORT (ACTUAL SIZE)

$1\frac{3}{4}$″

STEP $\frac{3}{8}$″ $\frac{3}{8}$″ $\frac{1}{8}$″

6.

STAND

$1\frac{3}{4}$″

$2\frac{5}{8}$″

$1\frac{3}{8}$″

SINGLE TREE

AXLE

$\frac{5}{8}$″ $3\frac{1}{2}$″

$\frac{3}{16}$″

5. Make the two body supports and glue them to the shafts ½″ back of the front crosspiece. Glue the upper crosspiece to these supports ¼″ in from the rear end. Make the steps and set them into pinholes made in the shafts.

6. Hang the body to the front crosspiece and the upper crosspiece with the leather straps which go around the crosspieces and are cemented together to form loops. Wire staples may be put in the underside of the floor and the straps passed through the staples, or the straps can be cemented to the bottom of the body. Hang the single tree from the front crosspiece with a narrow strip of leather. Make the wheels and hold in place with wooden washers. Make the stand and slide it over one shaft.

THE CONESTOGA WAGON

THE CHIME of the bells fastened above the necks of the horses and the rumble of the sturdy wheels of the Conestoga wagons were familiar sounds along the highways of America during the last part of the eighteenth and the first half of the nineteenth century. Thousands of these brightly painted freight carriers moved slowly along the roads drawn by sleek, powerful horses which were driven by a teamster with a whip under his arm and a "stogie" in his mouth. It is believed that the first of these wagons was built in the Conestoga Valley in Pennsylvania and received its name from the valley. These picturesque and distinctively American vehicles, with their curved bottoms and white canvas covers, were invariably painted red and blue and could carry five or six tons of freight. They played an important part in the history of America, helping to link our great country together at a time when there were no other means of long distance transportation. During the Revolution they were used to carry supplies to the American forces, and later to carry the settler and his family to the new lands of the West, in which period they were known as the prairie schooner.

Materials:

2 pc ⅛" x 2" x 9½"—sides
1 pc ³⁄₁₆" x 1¾" x 2½"—front end
1 pc ³⁄₁₆" x 2" x 2½"—back end
1 pc ¹⁄₃₂" x 2⅜" x 8¾"—bottom
} box

2 pc ⅛" x ⅛" x 9½"—A
2 pc ⅛" x ⅛" x 9"—B } sides
14 pc ¹⁄₁₆" x ¹⁄₁₆" x 1⅞"—C
} strips to strengthen box
2 pc ⅛" x ⅛" x 3"—A
2 pc ⅛" x ⅛" x 2⅝"—B } ends
8 pc ¹⁄₁₆" x ¹⁄₁₆" x 1¾"—C

1 pc ¼" x ⅜" x 5"—axle
1 pc ¼" x ¼" x 2½"—sand board
1 pc ¼" x ⅜" x 2¾"—bolster } front axle assembly
2 pc applicator 1" long—bolster stakes
1 straight pin

1 pc ¼" x ⅜" x 5"
1 pc ¼" x ¼" x 2½"
1 pc ¼" x ¼" x 2¾"—bolster } rear axle assembly
2 pc applicator 1" long—bolster stakes

1 pc ¼" x ¼" x 7½"—tongue
2 pc ³⁄₁₆" x 1" x 4½"—tongue holders } tongue assembly
1 pc ¹⁄₁₆" x ⅛" x 2¾"—fifth wheel

1 pc ³⁄₁₆" x ¼" x 6"—reach
2 pc ⅛" x 1" x 4"—reach braces
9 pc no. 2 reed about 9" long—bows (Or broom straws or pieces of wood ¹⁄₃₂" x ⅛" x 9")

2 pc $\frac{1}{16}''$ x $\frac{1}{2}''$ x $\frac{3}{4}''$—ends ⎤
2 pc $\frac{1}{16}''$ x $\frac{1}{2}''$ x $2\frac{1}{8}''$—sides ⎬ feed box
1 pc $\frac{1}{8}''$ x $\frac{1}{2}''$ x $2''$—bottom ⎦
1 pc $\frac{1}{2}''$ x $1''$ x $\frac{7}{8}''$—tool box
2 12 spoke wheels $2\frac{3}{4}''$ in diameter with $\frac{5}{8}''$ hubs $1''$ long
2 12 spoke wheels $2\frac{1}{4}''$ in diameter with $\frac{5}{8}''$ hubs $1''$ long
20 gauge wire for staples

1. Draw a line across one board, from which the side is to be made, $2''$ from each end. Then trace the drawing on a piece of paper and cut out the pattern. Place the pattern on the board so that the straight end of the pattern coincides with the line drawn across the board and the upper edge coincides with the edge of the board. Make the other end in the same way. When one side is cut out use that as a pattern for the other side. Hold the two sides together in the vise and sandpaper them so that they are exactly alike. With sandpaper make the upper and lower edges slightly curved as shown. Cut out the two end sections. Make lines or grooves with an awl lengthwise on the sides and ends about $\frac{3}{8}''$ apart to represent the boards. Glue or peg the sides to the ends.

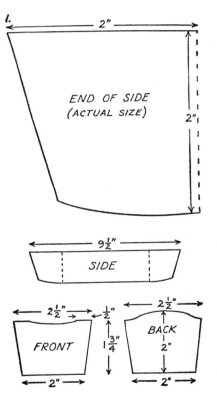

2. Glue the A pieces along each side flush with the top edges of the box. Glue seven of the C pieces along the sides of the box about 1¼″ apart. Fasten piece B lengthwise through the center of each side. File out notches in B so that it will fit over the C pieces. Put the reinforcing strips on the two ends in the same way. Allow endpieces A and B to extend over the ends of the side-pieces A and B. Cut off the lower ends of the C pieces so that they are even with the lower edges of the box. Make 36 wire staples, 18 for each side, and insert them into the A and B pieces about 1″ apart. Glue the bottom on. Hold with rubber bands until set. Put in the bows. If reed is used, flatten it by squeezing it between the jaws of the vise.

3. Make the front and rear axle assemblies as shown in the drawings. Round off the ends of the axles so that they are a little less than ⅛″ in diameter. Make notches in the axles for the tongue and reach braces. Drill no. 52 holes ⅛″ in from each end of the bolsters for the stakes, which should be tapered at the lower end.

2.

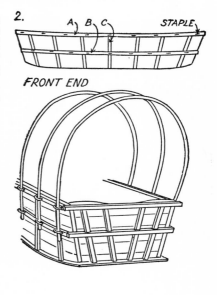

FRONT END

3.

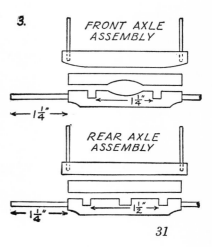

FRONT AXLE ASSEMBLY

REAR AXLE ASSEMBLY

4. Saw out the reach braces. Peg the braces to the reach about 3¾″ from the rear end. Set the ends of the reach and the braces into the notches cut out of the rear axle. Peg the bolsters to the axle.

5. Make the tongue holders and peg them to the tongue. Make two bands from flattened wire and put around the tongue and holders. Put the holders through the notches cut in the front axle. The back end of the tongue should be about 1″ in front of the axle. Fasten the fifth wheel to the ends of the tongue holders. Peg the sand board to the axle. Set the front end of the reach in the notch made in the center of the front axle, with the fifth wheel beneath the reach. Drill a pinhole down through the bolster, sand board, tongue and axle for a pin upon which the front axle will pivot.

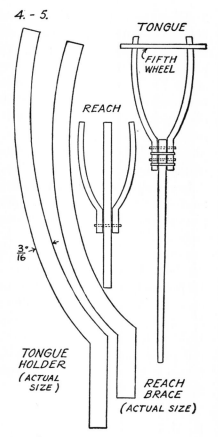

4. - 5.

TONGUE

FIFTH WHEEL

REACH

3″/16

TONGUE HOLDER
(ACTUAL SIZE)

REACH BRACE
(ACTUAL SIZE)

6. Make the wheels. Drill ⅛" holes through the hubs and hold them on the axles with wooden washers or ⅜" buttonmolds. Make the tool box and glue it to the right side. Fasten the ends of the feed box to the ends of the bottom piece. Glue on the sides. Glue the box to the rear end or hang it with pieces of small chain. Make a neck yoke and whipple trees for the wagon. Make the cover from a piece of unbleached muslin about 9" wide and 12" long. Hem the sides and ends. Run a string through the end hems and tighten over bows. Fasten edges to staples with thread.

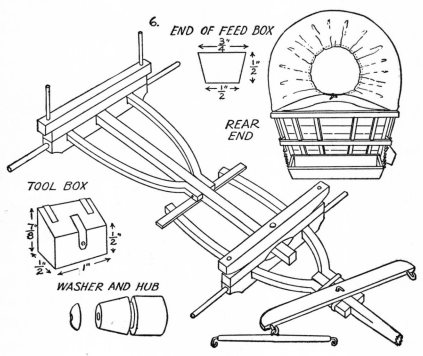

6.
END OF FEED BOX

REAR
END

TOOL BOX

WASHER AND HUB

THE CONCORD COACH

DURING THE NINETEENTH CENTURY the Concord Coach, one of the best known and most widely used of American vehicles, was made in the little town of Concord, New Hampshire. These sturdily built coaches, made of carefully selected hardwood, swayed along the roads of America during the eighteen hundreds on their strong leather thorough braces, which served as springs. There were seats for nine passengers in the Concord Coach, with room on the top and in the rear for the passengers' luggage. Thousands of these coaches were made in the carriage shops of New England and they, like the Conestoga wagons, played an important role in the expansion of the United States to the west.

Materials:

3 pc ¾₁₆″ x ¼″ x 5¾″—supporting beams
1 pc ¾₁₆″ x ¼″ x 2¾″—rear crosspiece
1 pc ¾₁₆″ x ¼″ x 2½″—front crosspiece
1 pc ¾₁₆″ x ¼″ x 3″ ⎤
2 pc applicator 1¼″ long ⎦ back axle
1 pc ¾₁₆″ x ⅜″ x 3″—rear bolster
2 pc ¾₁₆″ x ½″ x 3″ ⎤
2 pc applicator 1¼″ long ⎦ front axle and bolster
1 pc ¾₁₆″ x ¼″ x 7½″—tongue ⎤
2 pc ¾₁₆″ x ⅝″ x 3″—braces ⎥ tongue
1 pc ⅛″ x ½″ x 2½″—for fifth wheel ⎥ assembly
1 pc ¾₁₆″ x ¾₁₆″ x ½″—for fifth wheel to rub against ⎦
2 pc ⅛″ x ¼″ x ½″—rod holders ⎤
1 pc 14 gauge wire 5″ long—rod and lever ⎥
1 pc applicator 4″ long—brake beam ⎬ brake
2 pc ¾₁₆″ x ¼″ x ½″—shoes ⎥
2 pc 18 gauge wire ½″ long—hangers ⎦
2 12 spoke wheels 3″ in diameter with ⅜″ hubs ¾″ long—rear
2 12 spoke wheels 2½″ in diameter with ⅜″ hubs ¾″ long—front
4 pc ¼″ dowel ⅛″ long—washers
18 gauge wire for thorough brace posts
2 pc thin leather ⅛″ x 10″ long—thorough braces
2 pc ⅛″ x 3″ x 4½″—sides ⎤
2 pc ¾₁₆″ x 2″ x 2¼″—end crosspieces ⎥
1 pc ¾₁₆″ x 2½″ x 2¼″—floor crosspiece ⎥
4 pc balsa ¹⁄₃₂″ x 2½″ x 2½″—covering for ends ⎥
    and bottom ⎥
1 pc ⅛″ x 2½″ x 4⅝″—roof ⎬ body
8 pc applicator ⅝″ long—posts for railing ⎥
2 pc 18 gauge wire 4¾″ long—railing ⎥
2 pc 18 gauge wire 4⅜″ long—railing ⎥
4 pc 18 gauge wire 2¼″ long—railing ⎥
5 pc ¾₁₆″ x ¾₁₆″ x 2″—to protect end of body ⎦

2 pc ⅛″ x ⅞″ x 2¼″—bottom ⎫
2 pc ⅛″ x ⅝″ x 2¼″—front ⎬ end seats
2 pc ⅛″ x ¾″ x 2¼″—back cushion ⎭

2 pc ⅛″ x ½″ x 1″ ⎫
1 pc ⅛″ x ½″ x ¾″ ⎪
3 pc applicator ¾″ long ⎬ middle seat
2 pc applicator ¼″ long ⎭

2 pc ⅛″ x 1⅜″ x 1¼″—ends ⎫
1 pc ⅛″ x 1⅛″ x 1¾″—back ⎪
1 pc ⅛″ x 1″ x 1¾″—crosspiece ⎪
1 pc 1⁄16″ x 1⅛″ x 2¼″—seat ⎪
1 pc 3⁄16″ x 1⅝″ x 1¾″—floor piece ⎬ driver's seat
1 pc 1⁄16″ x ⅝″ x 2″—footpiece ⎪
1 pc 3⁄16″ x ¾″ x 2″—dash ⎪
2 pc 20 gauge wire 2½″ long—braces ⎪
2 pc 20 gauge wire 1⅝″ long—seat ⎪
2 pc 20 gauge wire ½″ long—railing ⎭

3 pc 3⁄32″ x 3⁄32″ x 1¾″ ⎫
4 pc 1⁄16″ x 1⁄16″ x 2″ ⎪
1 pc applicator 2¼″ long ⎬ luggage rack
4 pc thin leather 3½″ long ⎭

1 pc applicator ⅜″ long—whip socket
2 pc ⅛″ x ⅛″ x ¼″ ⎫ lamps
2 large round-headed pins ⎭
1 pc thin leather 6″ long—body strap
6 pc thin copper foil ⅛″ x ¼″—hinges
4 straight pins
Black cloth or thin paper for curtains
2 pc 18 gauge wire 2½″ long ⎫
2 pc 18 gauge wire 2″ long ⎬ steps
2 pc 18 gauge wire ⅝″ long ⎭
1 pc ⅝″ x ¾″ x 1¼″—trunk

1. Make the front axle and bolster as shown in the diagrams. Drill no. 45 holes ¾″ apart in the bolster and enlarge to about ³⁄₁₆″ x ¹⁄₁₆″ with the handle end of a file. Drill two ⅛″ holes 1″ apart in the axle and enlarge to ³⁄₁₆″ x ³⁄₁₆″. Make the notches in the rear bolster ³⁄₁₆″ x ¼″ and in the front crosspiece ³⁄₁₆″ x ⅛″. Drill no. 45 holes ¼″ deep in the ends of the axles, ⅛″ up from the lower edge, for the pieces of applicator.

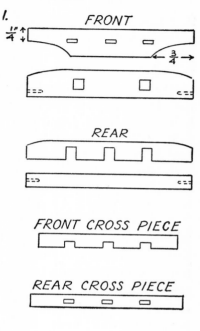

2. Shape both ends of the three beams as shown. Insert the beams into the openings made in the front bolster and the rear crosspiece. Set the beam assembly on the rear axle and peg the rear bolster over the beams to the axle. Allow the ends of the beams to extend about $\frac{5}{8}''$ behind the axle. Glue the front crosspiece over the beams $\frac{1}{2}''$ back of the front bolster.

3. Make the holders for the brake lever and glue them to the top of the two outside beams between the front axle and the front crosspiece. Put the brake hangers in pinholes made $2\frac{1}{4}''$ and $2\frac{1}{2}''$ in from the back ends of the two outside beams. Install the brake lever, beam and shoes.

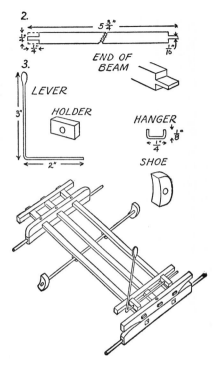

4. Make the tongue and tongue holders. Fasten the tongue between the holders with pins. Insert the holders through the openings made in the front axle and fasten the fifth wheel ¼" in from the ends of the holders. Glue the piece for the fifth wheel to rub against to the underside of the middle beam 1" back from the front axle. Drill a pinhole down through the center of the front bolster and front axle for the pin on which the front axle will pivot.

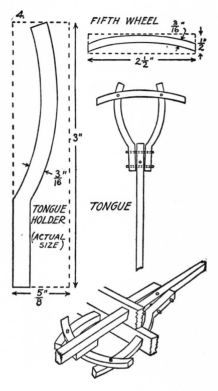

5. Make the posts from 1½″ pieces of wire and the braces from 1¼″ pieces from which to hang the thorough braces. Insert the front posts in pinholes made in the axle ⅜″ in from the ends. Set the back posts in holes made in the back crosspiece ⅜″ from the ends. The back braces should be set into the bolster and the front braces into the front crosspiece in line with the posts. Flatten the upper part of the posts and braces before bending. The upper end of the posts should be about 1″ above the bolster and rear crosspiece. Put steps made from 1″ pieces of wire into pinholes made ⅛″ in from the ends of the front bolster. Cement each thorough brace together so as to make it double and five inches long. Make loops from fine wire and put them through the braces. Hang them from the posts by these loops.

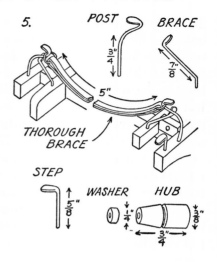

Construct the wheels and hold them on the axles with small buttonmolds or washers.

6. Cut out the sides and make the window and door openings. (Use a small soup can to get the curved shape of the body.) Cut out the doors very carefully with a sharp pointed knife. Peg the sides to the crosspieces. Cover with thin balsa. Have the

grain of the wood run crosswise to the body. Hold with rubber bands until set. The body may be covered with gummed tape such as is used to seal up packages instead of with balsa. Glue the strips to protect the back end of the body crosswise to the end about ⅜″ apart. Make small wire staples and insert them in pinholes made in the underside of the body midway between the ends and ⅛″ in from the sides. These staples will hold the body strap.

Round off the edges of the roof piece. Drill no. 45 holes ¼″ in from the sides for the railing posts through which no. 60 holes have been drilled ⅛″ and ⅜″ down from the top. Bend the top section of the railing to shape and put the pieces through the holes. Cement the crosspieces to the lengthwise pieces. The bent end of the top section will serve as a handle.

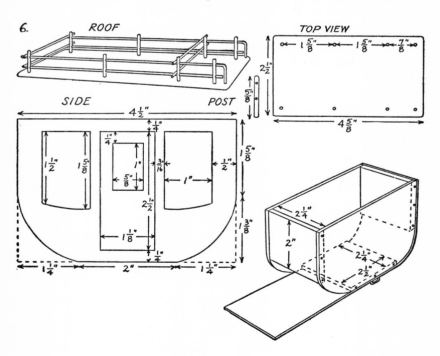

7. Assemble the driver's seat by gluing the ends to the back and floor piece, and the crosspiece between the ends flush with the top edges. Glue the seat board to the crosspiece. Shape the dash with sandpaper and a knife, and glue it to the footpiece. Then fasten the footpiece and dash to the floor board. Glue the seat to the front end ½″ down from upper edge. Insert the wire braces and seat railings into holes made in the end of the body and through the ends of the footpiece and seat board. Make steps from ½″ pieces of wire and insert in pinholes made in the ends of the seat.

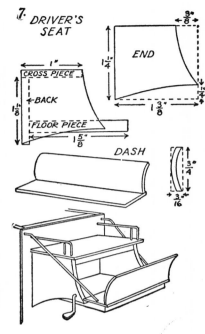

8. To make the inside end seats, fasten the seat board to the front piece. Glue the seats to the floor and to the ends of the coach. Glue the back cushion, which should be rounded off, to the ends of the body ¼" above the seats. Make the middle seat and put the middle leg into a no. 45 hole made in the center of the floor. The seats will pivot on the short pieces of applicator.

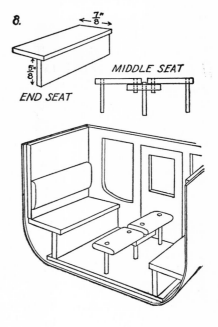

END SEAT

MIDDLE SEAT

9. Construct the luggage rack and hang it from the back end of the coach with the leather strips, which should be fastened just below the roof with small staples made of wire. Also glue the front ends of the rack to the body. Make imitation curtains for the windows and luggage carrier by rolling thin black paper or leather around a piece of applicator or wire. Hang them with narrow paper loops glued to the upper edge of the sides and back.

10. Make the lamps and push them into the sides of the body $\frac{1}{8}''$ back from the front end and $\frac{3}{4}''$ down from the top. Glue the whip socket to the right side just in front of and below the lamp. Construct the steps as shown in the drawing and put them into pinholes made in the center of the sides below the doors. Make the door handles from a $\frac{1}{4}''$ piece of wire and the imitation hinges from copper foil or tin bent to shape around a pin. Cement the "hinges" to the body. Insert $\frac{1}{2}''$ pieces of pin up through and down through the sides and into the doors. The doors, which open toward the front, will swing on these pins.

Glue on the roof. Set the body on the thorough braces and put the body strap through the staples in the underside of the body and under the middle beam. Make a set of whipple trees and a neck yoke, also a small trunk for the luggage rack.

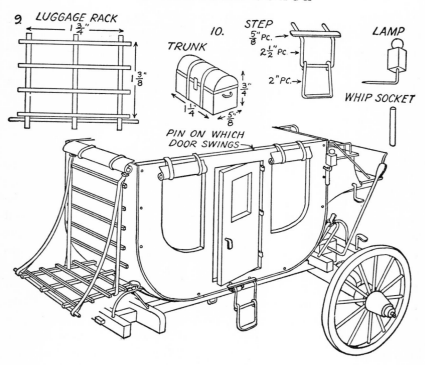

9. LUGGAGE RACK
1 3/4"
1 3/8"

10.
TRUNK
1 1/4"
3/4"
5/8"

STEP
5/8" PC.
2 1/2" PC.
2" PC.

LAMP

WHIP SOCKET

PIN ON WHICH
DOOR SWINGS

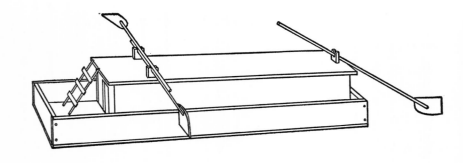

A RIVER FLATBOAT

FOR FORTY YEARS or more after the framing of our Constitution thousands of men, women and children moved westward in search of better land and new homes in the wilderness. Many of those hardy pioneers traveled to Pittsburgh in covered wagons and then floated down the Ohio and Mississippi Rivers on flatboats which they bought at the river's edge or made for themselves. There were many types of boats used, but the most common one was the flatboat which is shown here. The boat, which drifted slowly down the river at the mercy of the winds and currents, was steered by a long sweep, and large oars were used to help move the boat along on its journey down the river. Thousands of these boats floated down the rivers carrying the pioneers with all of their furniture, tools, cows, horses, chickens, and pigs. The family wash waved in the wind while often children played on the roof as the boats drifted toward their destination. When the end of the journey was at last reached the boat was broken up and sold for lumber as it could not be propelled upstream again.

Materials:

2 pc ¹⁄₁₆″ x ¾″ x 8″—sides ⎫
2 pc ⅛″ x ¾″ x 2″—ends ⎬ hull
1 pc ¹⁄₁₆″ x 2⅛″ x 8″—bottom ⎭
2 pc ¹⁄₁₆″ x 1½″ x 6″—sides ⎫
2 pc ⅛″ x 1½″ x 1¾″—ends ⎬ cabin
1 pc ¹⁄₁₆″ x 2⅛″ x 6¼″—roof ⎭
3 pc applicator 6″ long ⎫
3 pc ¹⁄₃₂″ x ½″ x 1″ ⎬ sweeps
3 pc ⅛″ x ⅜″ x ⅜″—holders for sweeps
2 flat toothpicks ⎫
3 pc ¹⁄₃₂″ x ¹⁄₁₆″ x ¾″ ⎬ ladder

1. Prepare the parts for the hull and cabin as listed. Cut an opening 1¼" x ½" in each of the end sections for doorways. Glue the sides of the cabin to the ends. Glue on the roof. Glue the sides of the hull to the ends and put on the bottom.

2. Make the notches in the sweep holders with a file. Put the two front holders ⅛" in from the edge of the roof and 1" from the front end of the roof. Place the other holder in the center of the roof ¼" back from the rear end. Make the sweeps.

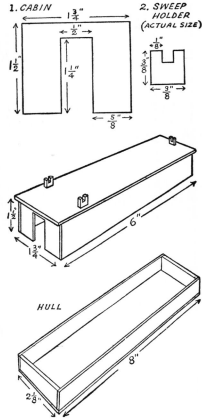

3. SWEEP AND LADDER

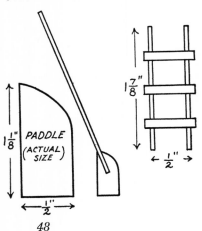

3. Make the ladder and lean it against the roof as shown in the drawing.

THE CLERMONT

ONE DAY in August of 1807 a large crowd of people gathered along the banks of the Hudson River to witness the start of the historic voyage of Robert Fulton's steamboat, *Clermont,* from New York City to Albany. The *Clermont,* sometimes called "Fulton's Folly," was a strange-looking craft as she slowly chugged up the Hudson on that autumn day, belching forth smoke and fire which frightened the onlookers who lined the river banks. The *Clermont* was not the first steamboat, for several others had been built and successfully operated before that eventful day. Robert Fulton knew about many of the experiments and inventions of those other men, among whom was John Fitch, sometimes called the real inventor of the steamboat. Robert Fulton, however, built the first steamboat which was a financial success, and he is remembered as the man who did much to revolutionize travel and commerce by water.

The *Clermont* heralded the beginning of a new era in transportation. With it the age of the steamboat arrived.

Materials:

1 block balsa 1½" x 2" x 16"—hull
2 pc balsa ³⁄₃₂" x ³⁄₃₂" x 17"—railing for sides
1 pc balsa ³⁄₃₂" x ³⁄₃₂" x 1¼"—railing for end
32 pc applicator ½" long or 32 pc ⅛" x ⅛" x ½"—posts for railing
2 pc ¹⁄₁₆" x ¹⁄₁₆" x 8¼"—inner railing
1 pc ¹⁄₁₆" x ¹⁄₁₆" x 1¼"—inner railing
1 pc ⅛" x ¼" x ¾"—stem
1 pc ¹⁄₁₆" x ½" x ¾"—rudder
1 pc applicator 2" long—rudder shaft
1 pc toothpick ⅝" long—tiller
1 pc ¼" x 1" x 3"—rear deckhouse
1 pc ¼" x 1" x 1¼"—front deckhouse
1 pc ¹⁄₃₂" x 1⅛" x 3⅛"—roof rear deckhouse
1 pc ¹⁄₃₂" x 1⅛" x 1⅜"—roof front deckhouse
1 pc ¾" dowel 3" long—boiler ⎫
1 pc ¼" dowel 3¼" long—smokestack ⎬ engine
1 pc ⅛" dowel ½" long—valve ⎭
1 pc ⅛" dowel 7" long—mainmast
1 pc ⅛" dowel 5½" long—mizzenmast
1 pc applicator 6½" long—yard
2 pc applicator 3" long—gaff and boom

4 discs ⅟₁₆″ thick and 2″ in diameter (use plywood) ⎤
4 discs ⅟₁₆″ thick and 1⅛″ in diameter (use plywood) ⎟
2 pc ¼″ dowel ¼″ long (or pieces cut from a ⎟ paddle
    spool)—hub ⎟ wheels
16 pc ⅟₃₂″ x ¼″ x ⅝″—paddles ⎟
1 pc applicator 3¾″ long—shaft ⎟
2 buttonmolds ½″ in diameter ⎦
1 pc ⅟₁₆″ x ¾″ x 8″ ⎤ stand
2 pc ⅛″ x 1″ x 1¼″ ⎦
    20 gauge wire or straight pins—for hooks
    Fine, black or dark green thread for rigging

1. Trace the drawings for the two ends of the boat on the block of balsa. Work the hull down to shape with a knife and sandpaper. Allow the stern to overhang by about ½″. The dotted lines indicate the under part of the stern which is pointed. Measure in 4″ from each end and draw lines across the hull. Measure in ⅜″ along each line and draw lines lengthwise on the hull. Remove the wood inside this rectangle to a depth of about ¾″.

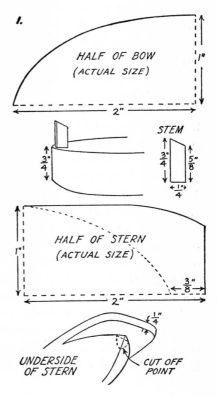

1.

HALF OF BOW
(ACTUAL SIZE)

1"

2"

STEM

¾

¾

⅝

¼

HALF OF STERN
(ACTUAL SIZE)

1"

2"

⅜"

¼"

UNDERSIDE
OF STERN

CUT OFF
POINT

2. Drill 16 no. 45 holes ¼″ deep along each side of the top of the hull about 1″ apart and ⅛″ in from the edges for the posts which hold the railing. Make the first hole 1″ back from the stem. Drill pinholes in every fourth or fifth post. If the square posts are used taper the lower end. Peg the railing to the stem and to the posts. Bend to shape over a flame if necessary. Put a piece of railing along the stern end between the side railings. Glue the inside railing along the sides and ends of the place cut out in the center of the boat.

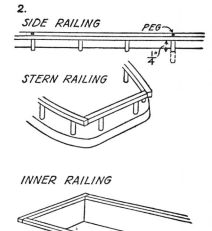

2.
SIDE RAILING   PEG
STERN RAILING
INNER RAILING

3. Shape the rudder and glue it to the shaft. Put the shaft up through a no. 45 hole made in the stern ⅜″ from the end. Insert the tiller into a no. 60 hole made in the upper end of the shaft. Glue the front deckhouse in place 1½″ back from the prow and the rear deckhouse 1″ in from the stern. Drill an ⅛″ hole in the rear deckhouse ½″ from the rear end and equidistant from the sides for the mizzen or rear mast. Drill another ⅛″ hole 3¼″ back from the prow for the mainmast.

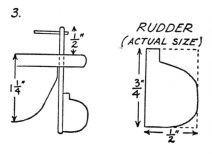

3.
RUDDER
(ACTUAL SIZE)

4. Drill no. 45 holes in the center of each 2″ disc. Trace the pattern for the paddle wheels on one of the discs and cut it out. Use this as a pattern for making the other three. Cut out 4 rings ⅛″ in diameter and ³⁄₃₂″ wide. Glue these rings to the spokes and center unit already cut out. Drill a no. 45 hole through the center of each hub. Glue a side assembly to each end of the hubs so that the holes coincide and the spokes are exactly opposite each other. Glue the paddles to the ends of the spokes so that when the wheel is turned forward the paddles will be on the surface of the spoke which enters the water first. Put the shaft through the holes made in the hull. Put the buttonmolds on the shafts next to the boat and put the assembled wheels on the ends of the shaft.

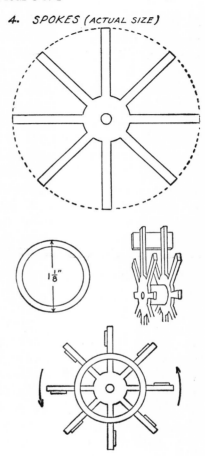

4. SPOKES (ACTUAL SIZE)

5. Drill a no. 60 hole ¾″ down from the top of the stack and assemble the engine. Flatten the lower side of the boiler and glue it to the hull with the stack toward the front end.

6. Drill a no. 60 hole 1¼″ down from the top of the mainmast and a similar hole ¾″ down from the top of the mizzenmast. Make narrow grooves around the mizzenmast 1″ and 4¼″ from the top in which the ends of the gaff and boom will fit. Use fine thread for the braces and rigging. Fasten the threads to the deck with little wire hooks. Run the braces for the stack and the masts through the holes made in them. Grooves made in the masts with a knife will keep the threads from sliding down. Lash the yard to the mast. Make the gaff and boom as shown. Drill pinholes ½″ in from the ends and run a thread up through the boom and the gaff and tie near the top of the mast. Make the stand and peg the model to it.

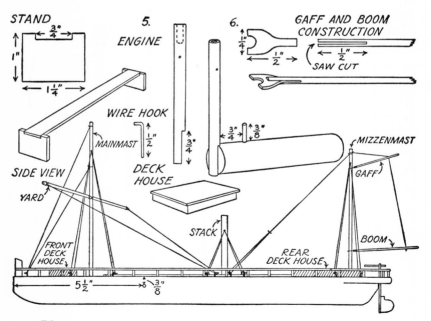

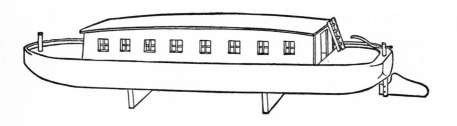

A CANAL PACKET

COMPLETION of the Erie Canal in 1825 marked another great step in the development of transportation in America. The story of the Erie Canal is a romantic one. The men who planned the canal were thinking of it as a means of carrying freight, but the people demanded passenger boats. Two types of boats were used for travel, the line boats which carried both freight and passengers, and the packets which provided only passenger service at a higher cost. Both types were usually sixty to eighty feet long and ten to twelve feet wide, although some of the earlier ones were narrower.

The packets were usually brightly painted in green, red, white or blue. In the bow of the boat was a small cabin for the crew members and behind that was the women's cabin. The largest compartment of all adjoined the women's cabin and served as a dining room and a general assembly room by day and as sleeping quarters for the men passengers at night.

Materials:

1 pc 1" x 2½" x 12"—hull
1 pc ⅛" dowel ¾" long—bitt or snubbing post
2 pc 3/16" x 1⅝" x 1¾"—ends
2 pc 1/16" x 1¾" x 8"—sides
1 pc 1/16" x 2" x 8"—floor
1 pc 1/16" x 2" x 8⅛"—roof
2 pc 3/16" x 1¾" x 1⅞"—partitions ⎫ cabin
2 pc celluloid or cellophane 1" wide and 7" long— ⎬
    windows ⎪
2 pc 1/32" x 1/32" x 7½"—window sash ⎪
16 pc 1/32" x 1/32" x 1"—window sash ⎭
2 pc 1/16" x ⅛" x 1¼"—sidepieces ⎫ ladder
4 pc toothpicks ½" long—rungs ⎭
1 pc 1/32" x ¾" x 1½"—rudder ⎫ rudder
1 pc ⅛" dowel 2¼" long—shaft ⎬ assembly
1 pc no. 2 reed or 14 gauge wire 1½" long—tiller ⎭
2 pc 3/16" x ¾" x 1½" ⎫ standard
1 pc 1/16" x 1" x 6" ⎭

1. Draw lines crosswise on the block of wood 2″ in from each end. Trace the drawing for one half of the bow on tracing paper. Fold the paper and cut out the pattern. Make the pattern for the stern the same way. Place the patterns on wood and draw around them. Work the hull down to shape. Draw a line all the way around the upper surface of the hull ⅛″ in from the edges except at the stern end where it should be ½″ in from the end of the hull. With a knife, cut along the line to a depth of about ³⁄₁₆″. Remove the wood inside of this line with a chisel to a depth of ³⁄₁₆″, except through the center of the boat between the lines drawn crosswise on the hull where the wood should be removed to a depth of about ½″. Sandpaper the inside of the hull until smooth.

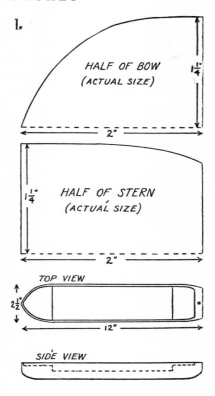

1.

HALF OF BOW
(ACTUAL SIZE)

$1\frac{1}{4}″$

2″

$1\frac{1}{4}″$

HALF OF STERN
(ACTUAL SIZE)

2″

TOP VIEW

$2\frac{1}{2}″$

12″

SIDE VIEW

2. Make the ½″ x ⅜″ openings for the windows ¾″ in from the lower edges of the two side sections and ½″ apart. Glue the two long pieces, to represent the window sash, lengthwise along the inside of each side section across the center of each window. Glue the short pieces the other way across each window. (Narrow strips of paper can be used instead of wood.) Then cement the cellophane or celluloid strips to the inside of each side section, or fasten with Scotch tape.

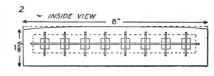

3. Saw out the ends and partitions as shown. Make the openings for the doors ½″ wide and 1¼″ high. Glue the end sections to the floor board equidistant from the sides. Glue one partition to the floor about 1¼″ from the front end section and the other partition about 3½″ from the front end and equidistant from each side of the floor. Glue or peg the sides to the ends and partitions. Put on the roof and shape the edges of the roof and floor to conform to the curve of the sides of the cabin. Set the completed cabin into the hull. Make the rudder assembly and put in place. Set the snubbing post into the

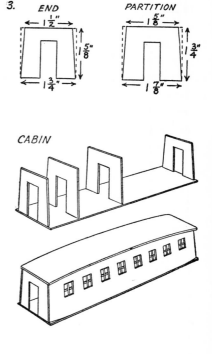

deck ½″ back from the prow. Make the standard and fasten to the bottom of the hull equidistant from the ends. Make the ladder and set against the rear end of the cabin.

Canal packets were often white with red or green trim. Paint the model and letter a name on the sides.

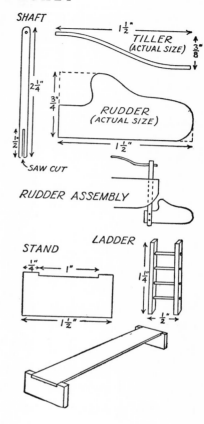

SHAFT

TILLER
(ACTUAL SIZE)

RUDDER
(ACTUAL SIZE)

SAW CUT

RUDDER ASSEMBLY

STAND

LADDER

A HORSE CAR

RAILROAD TRACKS, usually made of wood covered with thin strips of iron, were in use for many years before the development of steam-powered locomotives, and horses pulled wagons along the tracks long before the "iron horse" made its appearance.

The Baltimore and Ohio was the first railroad in America to carry passengers and freight. It used horses when it started its service in 1830 between Baltimore and Ellicott's Mills, now known as Ellicott City, Maryland—a thirteen-mile run.

The horse car was a box-like vehicle with three windows on each side and a door at the back, and was drawn by one horse. The driver sat perched on a seat at the front end of the car.

A HORSE CAR

Materials:

2 pc $\frac{1}{16}$″ x 2½″ x 5⅛″—sides

2 pc $\frac{3}{16}$″ x 1⅝″ x 2½″—ends

1 pc ⅛″ x 1¾″ x 6″—floor

1 pc ⅛″ x 2″ x 5¾″—roof

2 pc ⅛″ x ⅜″ x 4⅞″—seats

4 pc ⅛″ x ⅜″ x ½″—seat supports

1 pc $\frac{1}{16}$″ x ⅞″ x ⅞″—footrest

1 pc $\frac{1}{16}$″ x ½″ x ⅞″—driver's seat

4 pc $\frac{3}{16}$″ x $\frac{3}{16}$″ x ½″—axle holders

4 checkers about ¾″ in diameter—wheels (Or use wheels from an old toy locomotive or wooden discs $\frac{3}{16}$″ thick and ¾″ in diameter)

2 pc applicator 2⅜″ long—axles

1 round toothpick—single tree

2 pc 20 gauge wire 1¾″ long—rear step supports

2 pc 18 gauge wire ¾″ long—driver's seat supports

2 pc 18 gauge wire 1⅜″ long—footrest supports

1 pc 20 gauge wire 2½″ long—draw bar or hitch

1 pc applicator 2¼″ long—brake beam

2 pc ⅛″ x ⅛″ x ⅜″—brake shoes

1 pc 18 gauge wire 2⅜″ long—brake lever

2 pc 20 gauge wire ¾″ long—brake hangers

2 pc $\frac{1}{16}$″ x ⅛″ x ¼″—steps

1 pc $\frac{1}{16}$″ x ⅝″ x 1″—rear steps

1 pc 20 gauge wire ½″ long—handle

1. Cut out the openings for the windows ¼″ down from the upper edge of each side and ⅝″ apart.

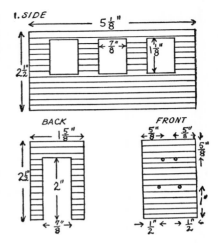

2. Cut out the opening for the door in one of the end sections (back). In the other end section (front) make holes with the pin drill for the brackets for the driver's seat and footrest. Glue or peg the sides to the ends.

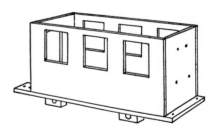

3. Saw out the opening in one end of the floor piece to form the place for the step. Bend the wires as shown and put them in pinholes made in the floor at A, B, C and D. The step will be cemented to these wire supports later. Also make holes at E and F for the hitch. The pinholes at G and H are for the brake holders.

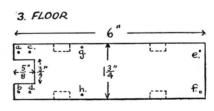

4. Make the axle holders by filing a notch in each of the pieces with a small round file. Glue the axle holders to the underside of the base 1¼″ from the ends of the floor. Glue on the floor section so that it extends ¼″ in front and ⅝″ in the back.

5. Bend the supports for the footrest and the driver's seat to the shape shown in diagram. First bend one end of each piece of wire over to a length of ⅛″. Then flatten the wire, except for the end which is bent over, before bending to the finished shape. Put the finished supports in the holes made in the front end of the car.

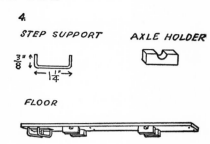

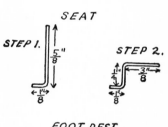

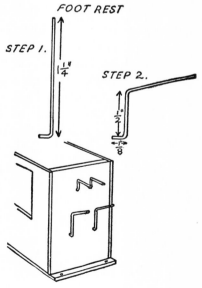

6. Make the seats and set them in place, one along each side of the car.

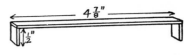

6. PASSENGER SEAT

$4\frac{7}{8}''$

$\frac{1}{2}''$

7. Make the hitch and put it into the holes made at E and F in the floor section. Also make a single tree 1″ long from a round toothpick. Put a small wire hook through the center.

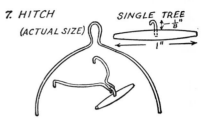

7. HITCH
(ACTUAL SIZE)

SINGLE TREE
$\frac{1}{8}''$
1″

8. Shape the roof board with sandpaper so that it is thinner at the sides and thicker in the middle to give the roof a slightly curved effect. Glue the roof in place so that the front end is even with the front end of the body. The roof will extend over the rear platform or step.

Cement the rear step, driver's seat and footrest, in which a slot has been cut, in place. Drill no. 45 holes in the center of the wheels and put them on the car.

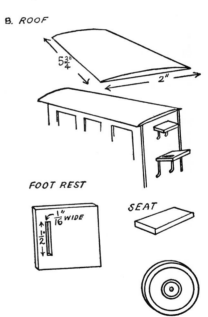

B. ROOF

$5\frac{3}{4}''$

2″

FOOT REST

$\frac{1}{16}''$ WIDE

$\frac{1}{2}''$

SEAT

64

9. Drill no. 45 holes through the center of each brake shoe. Put one shoe on each end of the brake beam and hang the beam from the underside of the floor with wire staples. Flatten one end of the brake lever. Insert the other end in a small hole made in the front end of the floor ½" in from the right side of the car. The lever will extend up through the slot cut out of the footrest.

Glue the steps to the right side of the car about ½" apart. Put the handle in small holes made about ½" above the top step.

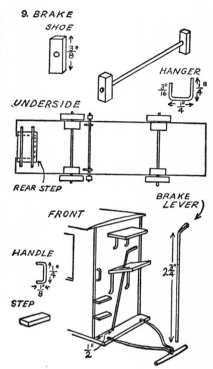

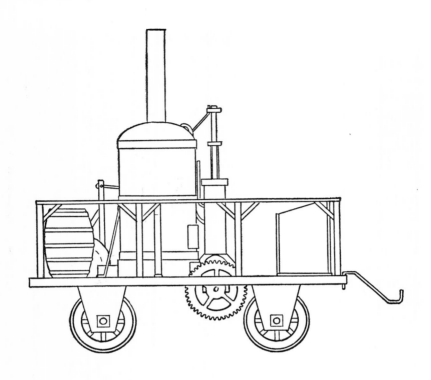

THE TOM THUMB

PETER COOPER, a New York business man, became interested in the Baltimore and Ohio Railroad, but believed that a steam locomotive should replace the horse. He went to Baltimore and built the Tom Thumb which, on an August day in 1830, ran a race with a horse-drawn car. The little "iron horse" lost the race due to a minor mechanical difficulty, but its performance convinced the railroad men that "steam power" would soon replace the horse on the railroad.

Materials:

1 pc $\frac{3}{16}''$ x 3" x 6$\frac{5}{8}''$—platform

12 pc $\frac{1}{8}''$ x $\frac{1}{8}''$ x 1$\frac{5}{8}''$—posts

24 pc $\frac{1}{16}''$ x $\frac{1}{16}''$ x $\frac{1}{2}''$—braces

2 pc $\frac{1}{16}''$ x $\frac{1}{8}''$ x 6$\frac{5}{8}''$—handrail sides

2 pc $\frac{1}{16}''$ x $\frac{1}{8}''$ x 2$\frac{5}{8}''$—handrail ends

2 pc $\frac{1}{8}''$ dowel 3$\frac{1}{4}''$ long—axles

4 checkers or discs or old toy locomotive wheels about 1" in diameter—wheels

4 pc $\frac{3}{16}''$ x 1" x 1"—axle holders

4 pc $\frac{3}{16}''$ x $\frac{1}{4}''$ x $\frac{1}{4}''$—journey boxes

1 pc balsa 2" x 2" x 5$\frac{3}{8}''$—boiler

1 pc balsa $\frac{1}{32}''$ x $\frac{3}{8}''$ x $\frac{1}{2}''$—fire door

1 pc balsa $\frac{1}{32}''$ x $\frac{1}{4}''$ x $\frac{1}{2}''$—ash door

3 pc thin copper foil or gold paper $\frac{1}{8}''$ wide and 5$\frac{1}{4}''$ long—bands

1 pc $\frac{1}{16}''$ x $\frac{1}{4}''$ x $\frac{3}{4}''$ (plywood best)—crank

1 pin

1 spool 2" long—cylinder

1 disc $\frac{1}{8}''$ thick and $\frac{3}{4}''$ in diameter—top of cylinder

2 pc applicator 1$\frac{3}{4}''$ long—guides

1 pc $\frac{1}{8}''$ dowel 2$\frac{1}{2}''$ long—piston

1 pc $\frac{1}{8}''$ x $\frac{1}{4}''$ x 1$\frac{1}{8}''$—cross head

1 pc $\frac{1}{8}''$ x $\frac{1}{4}''$ x $\frac{3}{4}''$—bracket

1 checker 1" in diameter—fan

1 pc $\frac{3}{16}''$ x $\frac{1}{4}''$ x 1"—tube from fan to boiler

1 pc $\frac{1}{8}''$ dowel 2" long—drive shaft

2 cog wheels from an old clock, one about 1$\frac{1}{4}''$ in diameter and one 1" in diameter, or saw out discs $\frac{1}{16}''$ thick and make notches in circumference

2 pc $\frac{1}{4}''$ x $\frac{1}{4}''$ x $\frac{1}{2}''$—drive wheel shaft holders

1 pc $\frac{1}{8}''$ dowel 1" long—pump cylinder

1 pc $\frac{3}{16}''$ x $\frac{1}{2}''$ x $\frac{1}{2}''$—base of pump

1 pc $\frac{1}{8}''$ x $\frac{1}{8}''$ x 2$\frac{1}{4}''$—upright post for pump rod

1 pc $\frac{3}{16}''$ x $\frac{3}{8}''$ x $\frac{1}{2}''$—base for post

1 pc $\frac{1}{16}''$ x $\frac{1}{8}''$ x $1\frac{3}{4}''$—brace for post

2 pc $\frac{1}{8}''$ x $1\frac{5}{8}''$ x $1\frac{5}{8}''$—end ⎤

1 pc $\frac{1}{16}''$ x $1\frac{1}{4}''$ x $1\frac{5}{8}''$—back ⎥

1 pc $\frac{1}{16}''$ x $1\frac{1}{4}''$ x $1\frac{3}{8}''$—front ⎥ wood box

1 pc $\frac{1}{16}''$ x $1\frac{1}{8}''$ x $1\frac{1}{4}''$—bottom ⎦

20 gauge copper wire for connecting rod, and pump rods

18 gauge wire for pipes

1. Cut the $1\frac{1}{2}''$ x $\frac{1}{4}''$ openings two inches in from the rear end of the platform as shown. Drill no. 60 holes for the pegs to hold the upright posts which support the handrail. Make these holes about $\frac{1}{8}''$ in from the ends and $\frac{1}{16}''$ in from the sides.

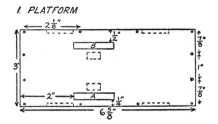

I. PLATFORM

2. Make the axle supports from ⅛″ wood and glue and peg them to the base 1″ from either end. Also glue the holders for the drive wheel shaft to the underside of the base ⅛″ from the inside edge of each of the openings cut in the base. The holders should be placed so that the shaft will be equidistant or ¾″ from each end of the openings. Put the wheels and axles in place. Make ⅛″ holes in the pieces which represent the journey boxes and glue them over the ends of the axles. Put the drive wheel on the 2″ shaft. Put the shaft through the holders, glued to the underside of the base, so that the top of the drive wheel extends up through opening B. Glue the crank to the end of the drive shaft. Insert a ¼″ piece cut from the head end of a pin in the other end of the crank over which the connecting rod will fit.

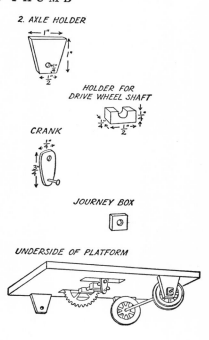

2. AXLE HOLDER

HOLDER FOR
DRIVE WHEEL SHAFT

CRANK

JOURNEY BOX

UNDERSIDE OF PLATFORM

3. Make the boiler from a block of balsa or soft wood 5⅜″ x 2″ x 2″. Work it down with a knife, file, and sandpaper to the dimensions given. Make a hole in the end of the smokestack. Cement the doors and the bands of thin copper or gold paper to the boiler. Glue the boiler to the base 1⅞″ from the front end and equidistant from the sides.

The boiler may also be made from a 3″ piece of round stick 1½″ in diameter, a 2″ piece of ⅜″ dowel for the stack, and a round block 1⅝″ in diameter and ⅜″ in thickness for the base. Round off the top of the boiler and drill a ⅜″ hole for the stack. Glue it to the base.

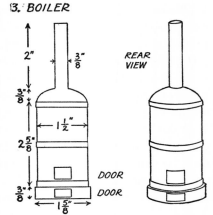

3. BOILER

4. Make the cylinder by chipping off one end of a spool and filing it so that it is round. Chip off the other end to make a base 1″ long and ½″ wide. Drill an ⅛″ hole through the center of the wooden disc and enlarge with a round file so as to allow the piston to slide up and down easily in the cylinder. Also drill no. 45 holes in the disc ½″ apart for the guides. Glue the disc to the top of the cylinder. Make the cross head and bracket as shown. Glue the piston rod into the cross head and the guides into the round disc. Set the piston and cross head in position and put the bracket on the guides. Glue the cylinder assembly to the platform so that the shaft of the cross head is directly above the shaft of the drive wheel. The long edge of the base of the cylinder should coincide with the inside edge of opening A.

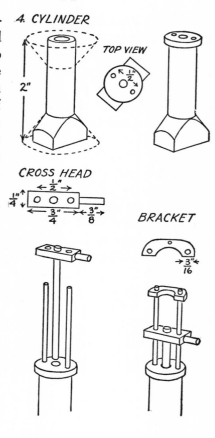

5. Make the cylinder of the pump from a 1″ piece of ⅛″ dowel which has a small hole drilled part way through it. (Or use a 1″ piece of plastic straw or corncob pipestem.) Drill a ⅛″ hole in the base of the pump and insert the piece of dowel into the hole. Drill a no. 60 hole through the cylinder of the pump just above the base for the pipe which will go from the boiler to the water barrel. Glue the pump to the platform so that it is ⅜″ in front of opening A and ⅛″ in from the edge of the platform.

Make a saw cut ¼″ deep in the upper end of the post. Glue the post assembly and brace to the platform ½″ in front of the pump and ⅛″ in from the edge of the platform. Drill a pinhole through the upper end of the post ⅛″ down from the top.

6. Make the fan and glue it to the platform just inside the upright post and brace.

7. Make the barrel from a block of balsa or other soft wood. Make it about 1½″ high and 1″ in diameter at the center. Use narrow strips of ⅛₂″ balsa for the bands around the barrel. Drill out the center to within ¼″ of the bottom to make it look more realistic. Make the wood box by cutting the two end sections as shown in the diagram. Glue the front and back sections to the ends. Glue on the bottom piece.

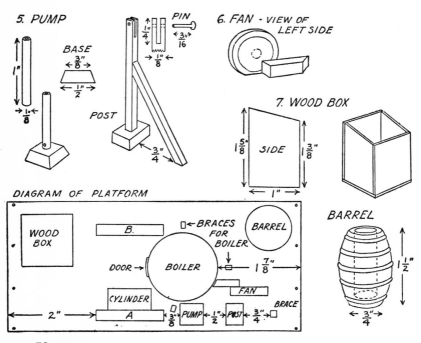

8. Make the connecting rod and the pump drive rod from 20 gauge wire. Put one end of the connecting rod over the pin in the crank and the other end over the shaft end of the cross head. Put the pump drive rod in position between the cross head and the upright post so that the wire piston moves up and down in the pump cylinder. Put the exhaust pipe in the hole made at A in the cylinder. Run a copper wire from hole B in the cylinder to hole B in the boiler. Run another wire from hole C in the boiler down and through the hole made in the cylinder of the pump and on around the fan to and into the barrel. Also run a wire brace from the hole made in the center of the bracket to the side of the boiler just above the pipe to the barrel. Brace the boiler with three braces 2" long. Flatten the wire and cement the braces to the boiler and to the platform.

9. Make the railing around the platform as shown. Drill no. 60 holes in the platform and in the center of the ends of each upright post. Peg or cement the posts to the platform and the handrail to the posts. Cut the ends of the braces at an angle and cement them to the posts and handrail.

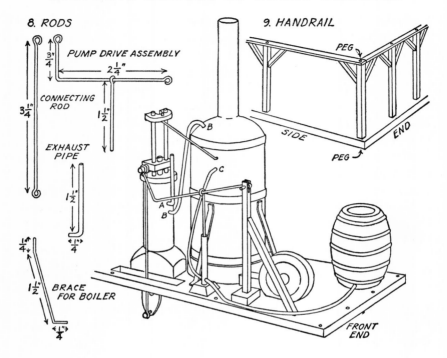

8. RODS

PUMP DRIVE ASSEMBLY
2¼"

CONNECTING
ROD
1½"
3¼"

EXHAUST
PIPE
1½"
¼"

¼"
1½"
BRACE
FOR BOILER
¼"

¾"

9. HANDRAIL
PEG
SIDE
END
PEG

B
C
A C
B
FRONT
END

THE MERRIMAC

THE UNITED STATES FRIGATE, *Merrimac*, rested at anchor in the Navy yard at Norfolk, Virginia, in the spring of 1861 when the Civil War began. To keep the *Merrimac* and other ships from falling into the hands of the Confederates orders were given to destroy them. The *Merrimac* was scuttled in the harbor where the water was shallow, and soon afterwards caught on fire and burned to the water's edge. The Confederates took possession of the Navy yard, put out the fires on the burning ships and later raised the *Merrimac* and some of the other ships abandoned by the Northerners. The *Merrimac* was then converted into an ironclad by the Confederates and about a year later, in March, 1862, caused great havoc among the wooden ships of the North in a battle off Newport News. The victory of the *Merrimac,* which had been officially renamed the *Virginia* by the Southerners but was still known as the *Merrimac,* plunged the North into gloom and dismay, and raised the hopes of the South for an early victory. But on the next night, when the destiny of the North and the South hung in the balance, another history-making ship, the little *Monitor,* steamed into Hampton Roads to challenge the supremacy of the mighty *Merrimac.* The battle was a draw, and the two ships never met in battle again. In May of that year, the *Merrimac* was blown up to prevent the Union Army from capturing her.

Materials:

 1 pc balsa or other soft wood ¾" x 2" x 11"—hull
 1 pc ¾" x 2" x 7½"—casemate
 1 pc ⅜" dowel ¾" long—smokestack
 1 buttonmold ⅜" in diameter—pilothouse
10 pc 18 gauge wire ⅜" long—guns
 2 pc 14 gauge wire ¾" long—funnels
 1 pc 14 gauge wire ⅜" long—ram
 1 straight pin—flagstaff

1. Draw the hull on the block of wood and work it down to shape.

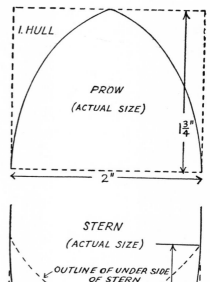

1. HULL

PROW

(ACTUAL SIZE)

$1\frac{3}{4}''$

2″

STERN

(ACTUAL SIZE)

OUTLINE OF UNDER SIDE OF STERN

1″

$\frac{1}{4}''$

2. To make the casemate draw a rectangle 5½″ long and 1″ wide on the top of the block of wood. Slant the sides and ends back to this rectangle. Then round off the ends. The finished length of the casemate should be 7″.

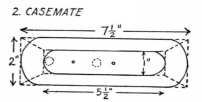

2. CASEMATE

$7\frac{1}{2}''$

2″

1″

$5\frac{1}{2}''$

3. Fasten the casemate to the hull 1¾" back from the prow. Drill a ¼" hole in the smokestack and glue it to the casemate 3" from the front end. Make the guns from ½" pieces of wire or small nails and put one in each end and four along each side. Glue a ⅜" buttonmold to the front end of the casemate for the pilothouse. Make the ventilators and set them in place.

Make a small Confederate flag and cement it to the staff at the stern of the ship. Insert a ¼" piece of 14 gauge wire or a nail into the prow for the ram.

Paint the model dark gray.

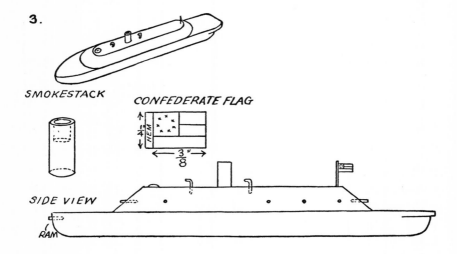

SMOKESTACK

CONFEDERATE FLAG

SIDE VIEW

RAM

THE MONITOR

THE *Monitor*, sometimes called a "cheesebox on a raft," was designed by John Ericsson and was completed early in the year of 1862. It was unlike any ship which had been built up to that time, because it had a revolving gun turret and was built low in the water. It was destined to revolutionize the navies of the world. The *Monitor* was much smaller than its antagonist the *Merrimac*, but could bring its guns into action quicker and more effectively. On that Sunday morning in March, 1862, when the *Merrimac* steamed out to complete the destruction of the helpless wooden warships of the North off Newport News, she was met by the strange-looking *Monitor* with her revolving turret inside of which were two eleven-inch guns. The epic battle between the two ironclads raged for some time, when suddenly the *Merrimac* withdrew and steamed away. The battle was not decisive, but the effects were far-reaching, for it proved that the day of the wooden warship had passed. The *Monitor* went down in a storm at sea in December, 1862.

Materials:

1 pc ³⁄₁₆″ x 1⅝″ x 7″—raft
1 pc ½″ x 1⅜″ x 5″—hull
1 disc about ⅜″ thick and ⅞″ in diameter—turret
1 pc applicator ½″ long—turret shaft
1 pc ¼″ x ¼″ x ¼″—pilothouse
2 straight pins—flagstaffs
2 nails or pieces of 18 gauge wire—guns
1 pc 18 gauge wire 1½″ long—rudder support
1 pc ¹⁄₁₆″ x ¼″ x ⅜″—rudder
1 pc applicator ¾″ long—propeller shaft
1 pc ⅜″ dowel ⅛″ long—propeller

1. Make the raft as shown in the diagram. Drill a no. 45 hole in the center for the turret shaft.

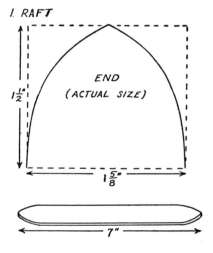

2. Draw a rectangle 4″ long and ⅞″ wide on the bottom of the piece of wood from which the hull is to be made. Make the sides and ends slant in to this rectangle.

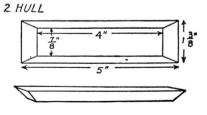

3. Put the turret shaft into a no. 45 hole made in the center of the turret. Set the guns into the turret about ⅛" apart and ⅛" from the lower edge.

3. TURRET AND PILOT HOUSE

4. Fasten the hull to the raft ¾" from the front end and equidistant from the sides. Drill a pinhole through the rudder and set the rudder assembly into a hole made in the end of the hull, or cement the rudder to the shaft. Make a no. 45 hole in the propeller and insert the shaft into a hole made in the hull just above the rudder shaft.

4. PROPELLER AND RUDDER

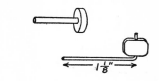

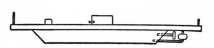

Glue the pilothouse to the deck 1¼" from the front end. Make little flags for the flagstaffs and put one at each end of the *Monitor.* Paint the model dark gray.

J. MACDONALD

AN EARLY BICYCLE—
THE ORDINARY

DURING THE DECADE between 1860 and 1870
when the Civil War was being fought in the United States,
a Frenchman attached cranks and pedals to the front wheel
of a velocipede and the bicycle was born. In those days
bicycles were known in America as "boneshakers" and for
good reason as they had heavy wooden frames and iron
tires. The front wheel of the early bicycle was sometimes
five feet in height while the rear wheel was small in com-
parison. This forerunner of the modern bicycle was called
"The Ordinary" and was usually ridden only by those of

an adventurous nature. To sit perched above the large front wheel, pedaling along a dirt roadway, was a feat for those who were willing to take a chance of being thrown head first to the ground. It was not until the 1880's that the modern bicycle was developed.

Materials:

1 pc $\frac{3}{16}$" x 1$\frac{1}{2}$" x 4$\frac{1}{2}$"—for beam
2 pc $\frac{1}{16}$" x $\frac{3}{4}$" x 4"—rear fork
1 pc $\frac{3}{16}$" x 1$\frac{1}{2}$" x 3$\frac{1}{8}$"—front fork
1 wooden embroidery hoop about 5" in diameter—front wheel
    (With a knife and file cut the hoop down to a width of $\frac{3}{16}$"
    or saw out a rim $\frac{1}{8}$" thick $\frac{3}{16}$" wide and 5" in diameter.)
1 wheel $\frac{1}{8}$" thick $\frac{3}{16}$" wide and 2$\frac{1}{2}$" in diameter—rear wheel
1 pc $\frac{3}{8}$" dowel $\frac{3}{4}$" long—front hub
1 pc $\frac{3}{8}$" dowel $\frac{1}{2}$" long—rear hub
16 pc applicator 2$\frac{1}{4}$" long—front spokes
12 pc applicator 1" long—rear spokes
2 pc $\frac{1}{16}$" x $\frac{1}{8}$" x 1"—crank arms
1 pc applicator 1" long—rear axle
1 pc metal $\frac{1}{32}$" x $\frac{1}{8}$" x 1$\frac{1}{4}$"—seat support (Tin is all right or
    flattened wire.)
1 pc $\frac{1}{8}$" x $\frac{1}{4}$" x $\frac{1}{4}$"—step
1 pc $\frac{1}{16}$" x $\frac{3}{4}$" x 1$\frac{1}{2}$"—seat
1 pc $\frac{1}{16}$" x $\frac{1}{4}$" x 2$\frac{1}{2}$"—handle bar
1 pc applicator $\frac{3}{4}$" long—steering post
2 pc toothpick $\frac{3}{8}$" long—pedal
1 pc $\frac{3}{16}$" x 1$\frac{1}{2}$" x 9"—base

1. Trace the beam on the wood and saw out. Drill a no. 45 hole down through the beam ¼″ from the front end. Shape the lower end of the beam as shown. Use a file.

2. Trace and saw out the two parts for the rear fork. Drill a no. 45 hole ⅛″ from one end. Drill both pieces together as the holes must be opposite each other. Glue the two pieces of the rear fork to the beam as shown. Make the step.

3. Cut out the seat and drill a no. 60 hole ⅛″ from the front end. Make the seat support as drawn.

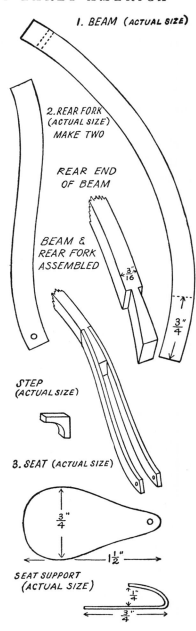

I. BEAM (ACTUAL SIZE)

2. REAR FORK (ACTUAL SIZE) MAKE TWO

REAR END OF BEAM

BEAM & REAR FORK ASSEMBLED

$\frac{3}{16}$

$\frac{3}{4}''$

STEP (ACTUAL SIZE)

3. SEAT (ACTUAL SIZE)

$\frac{3}{4}''$

$1\frac{1}{2}''$

SEAT SUPPORT (ACTUAL SIZE)

$\frac{1}{4}''$

$\frac{3}{4}''$

4. Trace and saw out the front fork. Drill a no. 45 hole down through the center of the upper end of the fork. File notches ⅛″ deep and ¹⁄₁₆″ in width in the lower ends of the two sides of the fork for the axle. Drill pinholes through the fork for pegs which will hold the axle in place.

4. FRONT FORK

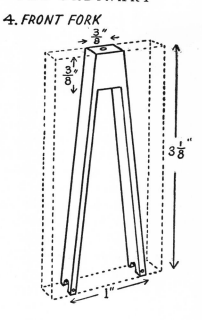

5. Shape the handle bars from a piece of wood ¹⁄₁₆″ x ¼″ x 2½″.

5. HANDLE BAR

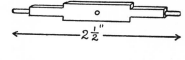

6. Make the pedal cranks by drilling a no. 45 hole near one end and a no. 60 hole near the other end. The larger holes will fit over the ends of the front axle. Insert a ⅜″ piece of toothpick in the smaller holes for the pedals.

6. PEDAL CRANK

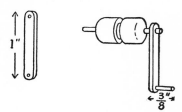

Make the wheels. Put 16 spokes in the front wheel and 12 spokes in the rear wheel.

Assemble the bicycle as follows: Insert a ¾″ piece of applicator in the hole in the upper end of the front fork. Fit the upper ends of the rear fork into the beam where it was filed out. Glue the step to the left side of the rear fork ¼″ down from upper end or joint. Cement the seat supports to the beam 1¼″ back from the front end. Peg or cement the seat to the beam ½″ back from the front end so that it rests on the curved part of the metal support.

Put some glue on the front axle and put it through the hub of the front wheel. It should extend ¼″ on each end of the hub. Set the axle and wheel into the fork so that the axle fits in the notches made in the fork. Fasten in place with small pegs. Put a crank on each end of the axle.

Set the rear wheel inside the fork and insert the axle. This wheel will revolve on the axle.

Set the beam on the front fork and put on the handle bars. The front wheel will pivot on the piece of applicator which goes through the beam.

Mount the bicycle on a piece ¾₁₆″ x 1½″ x 9″ with wire staples.

THE FIRST FORD

ONE NIGHT in April, 1893, the residents of Bagley Avenue in Detroit were aroused from their slumber by unusual sounds. Hurrying to their windows, they saw a tall man seated in a strange-looking vehicle which clattered down the street. That man was Henry Ford, one of America's pioneer automobile builders, and the strange vehicle with its bicycle wheels, buggy seat, and two cylinder engine was the Ford automobile, the first of millions of other Fords. It was a treasured possession of Henry Ford, the Michigan farm boy who became one of America's greatest industrialists.

Materials:

2 pc $\frac{3}{16}$" x $\frac{1}{4}$" x 5"
2 pc $\frac{3}{16}$" x $\frac{1}{4}$" x 6" } frame

1 pc $\frac{1}{16}$" x $1\frac{3}{4}$" x $2\frac{1}{4}$"—floor
2 pc $\frac{1}{8}$" x $1\frac{1}{4}$" x $1\frac{1}{2}$"—sides
1 pc $\frac{1}{16}$" x $1\frac{1}{4}$" x $2\frac{1}{4}$"—front end } body
1 pc $\frac{1}{8}$" x $\frac{3}{4}$" x 2"—partition

1 pc $\frac{1}{8}$" x $1\frac{1}{2}$" x $2\frac{1}{2}$"—back
1 pc $\frac{1}{8}$" x $1\frac{1}{8}$" x 2"—bottom
2 pc $\frac{1}{8}$" x $\frac{1}{2}$" x $1\frac{1}{4}$"—sides
1 pc $\frac{3}{16}$" x 1" x 2"—cushion } seat
2 pc metal $\frac{1}{32}$" x $\frac{1}{8}$" x 4"—supports
2 pc 20 gauge wire $1\frac{1}{2}$" long—braces
1 pc $\frac{3}{16}$" x $\frac{7}{8}$" x $1\frac{3}{4}$"—gasoline tank

1 pc $\frac{1}{16}$" x $\frac{3}{4}$" x $1\frac{1}{4}$"—base
1 pc $\frac{3}{8}$" x $\frac{3}{8}$" x $\frac{3}{4}$"—parts of engine
2 pc $\frac{1}{4}$" dowel 1" long—cylinders } engine
1 pc $\frac{1}{16}$" x $\frac{1}{4}$" x $1\frac{1}{2}$"—back crosspiece

1 disc or checker $\frac{1}{4}$" x $1\frac{1}{4}$" in diameter—wheel
1 pc $\frac{1}{2}$" dowel $\frac{3}{16}$" long—pulley } balance wheel
1 pc applicator 1" long—shaft

1 pc $\frac{3}{4}$" dowel $\frac{1}{2}$" long
1 pc applicator $2\frac{1}{2}$" long—shaft } clutch and
1 pc $\frac{3}{8}$" dowel $\frac{1}{8}$" long—sprocket wheel } counter shaft
1 pc $\frac{1}{2}$" dowel $\frac{1}{8}$" long—sprocket wheel on rear axle

1 pc $\frac{1}{8}$" x $\frac{1}{4}$" x 3"—axle
2 pc $\frac{1}{8}$" dowel 1" long
2 pc applicator $\frac{5}{8}$" long } spindles
2 pc 18 gauge wire 1" long—spindle arms } front axle and
1 pc $\frac{1}{16}$" x $\frac{1}{8}$" x $2\frac{3}{4}$"—tie rod } steering device
1 pc 18 gauge wire 6" long—tiller
1 pc $\frac{1}{8}$" dowel $\frac{3}{16}$" long—hand grip
1 pc $\frac{3}{32}$" x $\frac{3}{32}$" x $\frac{3}{8}$"—tiller holder
2 pc $\frac{1}{8}$" x $\frac{1}{2}$" x $1\frac{1}{4}$"—springs

2 pc ⅛″ x ⅛″ x ½″—body hangers
1 pc corncob pipestem or plastic straw about ³⁄₁₆″ in diameter
    and 2¾″ long—rear axle housing
1 pc applicator 3⅞″ long—rear axle
4 wheels 2¼″ in diameter with ⅜″ hubs ⅜″ long and 16 wire
    spokes (20 gauge wire or straight pins)
1 toothpick or pc of 18 gauge wire 1¾″ long—clutch lever
1 pc 18 gauge wire ½″ long—foot brake pedal
1 pc ¼″ dowel ¼″ long ⎫
1 large-headed pin   ⎬ headlight

1. Construct the frame as shown in the diagrams. Fasten the outside beams to the underside of the floor piece ¹⁄₁₆″ in from the edges, and the inner beams ⅜″ in from the outer beams. Cut the groove in the two longer beams, for the rear axle housing, with a round file. Set small wire staples, just large enough for a piece of applicator to go through, in the outside beams ½″ back from the floor board, and two staples in the inside beams 2¼″ back from the floor board. Glue the back crosspiece across the inner beams flush with the back ends.

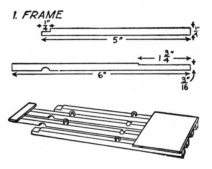

I. FRAME

2. Cut out the sidepieces and glue the front end to the ends of the sidepieces. Fasten the partition between the sides ⅜″ from the back edges and glue the body to the floor board even with the front edge. Glue the body hangers to the sides of the body midway between the front and back edges.

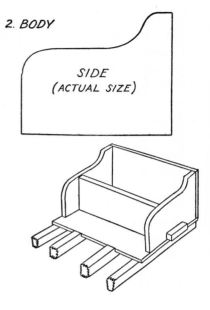

2. *BODY*

SIDE
(ACTUAL SIZE)

3. Assemble the engine. Make a groove with a file around the balance wheel pulley and glue it to the wheel. Drill a no. 45 hole through the center of the pulley and wheel for the shaft. Make two grooves ¹⁄₁₆″ apart around the clutch, and drill a no. 45 hole through the center. Cut notches around the circumference of the piece of ⅜″ dowel to make the sprocket wheel. Install the shafts and wheels. Run a narrow leather belt between the balance wheel pulley and the clutch.

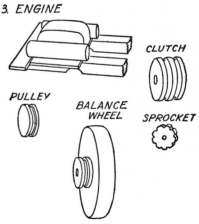

3. *ENGINE*

CLUTCH

PULLEY

BALANCE
WHEEL

SPROCKET

4. Make the seat. Glue the gasoline tank to the underside. Put the wire braces in pinholes made in the ends of the back ⅜" down from the top and in the side-pieces ¼" back from the front edge. Round off the edges of the cushion. Cement, or fasten with tiny nails or pins, the seat supports to the outside beams and the seat to the supports.

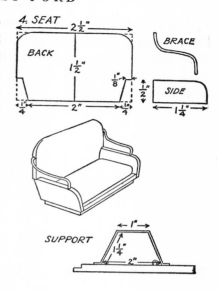

5. FRONT AXLE AND
        STEERING DEVICE

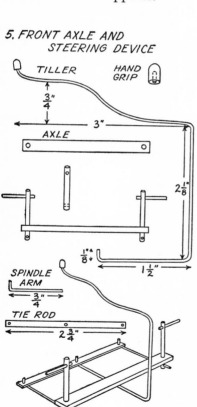

5. Construct the front axle and steering device as shown in the diagrams. When making the tiller bend the handle part first. Put the straight part down through a no. 60 hole made in the floor board just back of the dash and equidistant from the sides. Then make the bends in the lower end. Cement the hand grip to the end of the tiller.

6. Cut out the springs and glue them to the underside of the body hangers. Peg or glue front axle assembly to the lower side of the springs.

6. *SPRINGS - MAKE TWO*

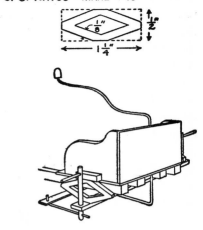

7. Glue the ½″ sprocket wheel on the rear axle ½″ from one end and put the axle into the housing.

7. *REAR AXLE*

SPROCKET WHEEL

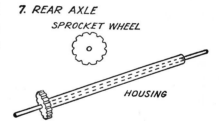

HOUSING

8. Make the wheels and put them on. Glue the back wheels to the axle which turns inside the housing. The wheels on the first Ford were bicycle wheels with wire spokes. Pins or 1″ pieces of wire should be used for spokes. When making these wheels, first saw out the discs and make 16 pinholes around the circumference. Round off the edges of the wheel and then saw out the inside. Drill a no. 45 hole through the center of the hub and a no. 60 hole through the hub in the opposite direction equidistant from the ends. Put a long pin or wire through one

8. WHEELS

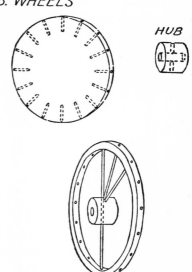

HUB

hole in the rim, on through the no. 60 hole in the hub and through the hole in the rim directly opposite the first one. Put the other spokes through the holes in the rim and into the hub just far enough to stay. Cut off the ends and with the hub in the vise, tap each spoke gently with a hammer until each spoke is flush with the rim. If pins are used for spokes blunt the ends by rubbing on a file so they will not split the hub. Do not push spokes into the hole made lengthwise in hub. When spokes are in place remove the first long pin or wire, cut in two and re-insert. Rubber bands can be used for tires.

Make a groove in the tiller holder and glue it to the front end around the tiller. Make the brake pedal and insert into a pinhole made in the floor. Insert a toothpick or a 1¾" piece of flattened wire into the floor just left of the tiller for the clutch lever. Make the lamp from a ¼" piece of ¼" dowel and a large-headed pin.

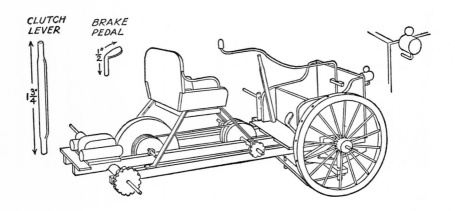

CLUTCH LEVER BRAKE PEDAL

THE FIRST AIRPLANE

MAN, down through the centuries, envied the birds as they soared through the heavens, and made many attempts to fly himself. Various types of flying machines were devised, but it was not until 1903, at Kitty Hawk, North Carolina, that a machine successfully carried a man into the air. That first flight lasted only a few seconds but the airship, built by Wilbur and Orville Wright, made man's dream of the conquest of the air come nearer realization. The first airship made by the Wright brothers, who were bicycle makers in Dayton, Ohio, was the result of years of study and of experimentation with gliders. An engine, which they made in their little shop in Dayton, was installed in a glider for the first historic flight. It was a crude craft as compared with our modern giants of the air, but it marked the beginning of a new era in transportation.

Materials:

2 pc balsa $\frac{3}{16}$" x $2\frac{1}{4}$" x $13\frac{1}{2}$"—planes
18 pc balsa $\frac{3}{32}$" x $\frac{3}{32}$" x $2\frac{1}{2}$"—struts
2 pc $\frac{1}{16}$" x 1" x 5"—horizontal rudder
8 pc balsa $\frac{1}{16}$" x $\frac{1}{16}$" x $1\frac{1}{4}$"—struts for horizontal rudder

2 pc $\frac{1}{16}$" x $\frac{3}{4}$" x 2"—sides
6 pc flat toothpick 1" long—struts
2 pc $\frac{1}{16}$" x $\frac{1}{8}$" x 1"—cross braces ⎬ vertical rudder
2 pc $\frac{1}{16}$" x $\frac{1}{8}$" x 4"—supports

2 pc $\frac{1}{8}$" x 2" x $8\frac{1}{2}$"—for runners (plywood best)
4 pc balsa $\frac{1}{8}$" x $\frac{1}{8}$" x 1"—struts
2 pc balsa $\frac{1}{8}$" x $\frac{1}{8}$" x $1\frac{1}{4}$"—braces
2 pc $\frac{1}{16}$" x $\frac{3}{8}$" x 3"—crosspieces
2 pc balsa $\frac{3}{32}$" x $\frac{3}{32}$" x $5\frac{1}{2}$"—braces from upper wing
2 pc balsa $\frac{1}{16}$" x $\frac{1}{8}$" x $5\frac{3}{4}$"—braces from front sled ⎬ sled
    struts to front end of sled
1 pc balsa $\frac{1}{16}$" x $\frac{1}{8}$" x $4\frac{1}{2}$"—lever arm to horizontal rudder
1pc flat toothpick $1\frac{1}{2}$" long—lever

2 pc $\frac{1}{8}$" x $1\frac{1}{2}$" x 2"—supports
2 pc 18 gauge wire 2" long—shafts
2 pc $\frac{3}{16}$" x $\frac{3}{8}$" x $2\frac{1}{2}$"—propellers ⎬ propeller assemblies
2 pc $\frac{1}{4}$" dowel $\frac{1}{8}$" long—pulleys

1 pc $\frac{3}{16}$" x $\frac{3}{8}$" x 1"
1 pc $\frac{1}{4}$" dowel $\frac{3}{4}$" long ⎬ tanks

1 pc $\frac{1}{4}$" x $\frac{1}{4}$" x $\frac{3}{4}$"—A
1 pc $\frac{1}{8}$" x $\frac{1}{8}$" x $\frac{1}{2}$"—B
2 pc $\frac{1}{16}$" x $\frac{1}{8}$" x $\frac{3}{4}$"—C ⎬ engine
1 pc $\frac{1}{4}$" dowel $\frac{1}{8}$" long—D

Fine black thread for braces

1. Shape the wings as shown. Each wing curves downward from the center to the ends. To make this curve, sandpaper away the center part of the underside of each wing. Then sandpaper down the upper side of each wing at the ends. Also make the front and back edges of each wing turn downward by sandpapering away the upper part of the wing along each edge. Do not make the wings too thin. Drill 9 no. 45 holes along the front edge of the upper wing. Put the holes ¼″ in from the front edge and 1⅝″ apart except for holes D and E which are 1¼″ apart and holes E and F which are 2″ apart. Start the first hole ¼″ in from one end of the wing. Measure back 1½″ from the front edge of the wing and make 9 more no. 45 holes for the rear struts. Make all of these holes 1⅝″ apart. Lay this wing on the lower wing and mark the location of the holes on the lower wing. Drill the holes in the lower wing. Taper each strut a little at the ends and insert them into the holes made in the wings. Allow each strut to extend above and below the surface of the wings. Do not cut off the ends of the struts until the thread braces are put in. The wings should be about 2″ apart at the center and 1⅞″ apart at the ends when finished.

I. WINGS

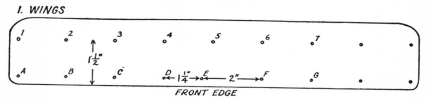

FRONT EDGE

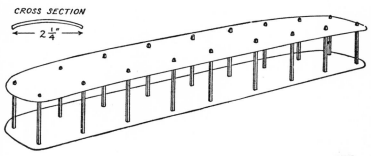

CROSS SECTION

2. Make the horizontal rudders. Cut out the two ⅛″ x ¼″ openings in the lower plane for the ends of the sled to go up through. Make the openings 2½″ apart. Drill no. 52 holes for the struts ⅛″ in from the edges. Join the two planes together with the struts so that they are about 1″ apart. Drill both planes together so as to have the holes exactly opposite each other.

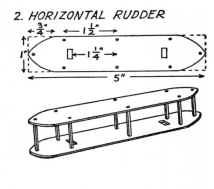

2. HORIZONTAL RUDDER

3. Make the vertical rudder. Drill no. 60 holes in the center of each of the crosspieces. Drill no. 58 holes for the toothpick struts.

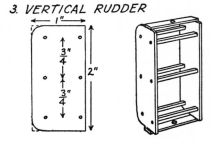

3. VERTICAL RUDDER

4. To make the propeller supports, first draw lines AB and CD on the piece of wood. Draw line AB equidistant from the ends and line CD ½″ in from one edge. Make a dot ⅛″ to either side of points A, B, C, D. Connect the dots with lines. Then draw inner lines about ⅛″ in from the outer lines. Cut out the support. Drill no. 60 holes through the propeller support at A and B for the propeller shaft. Buy two small propellers about 2½″ long or whittle them. Glue the propeller assemblies to the lower wings between rear struts 3 and 4 and 6 and 7. The propellers on this plane were on the back.

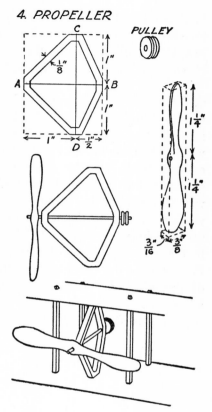

4. PROPELLER

PULLEY

5. Assemble the engine and glue to the lower wing midway between front struts D and E, with the pulley in line with the propeller pulleys. Glue the round tank to the upper part of front strut E and the other tank to the front strut D.

6. The best way to put the braces in is by threading a small needle with fine thread. Push the needle through strut A just beneath the upper wing, then to strut B just above the lower wing. Then on to strut C, D and so on. Complete the cross by coming back. Do the same with the rear struts and also the struts in the horizontal rudder. Secure the ends of the thread with cement or by winding them around a strut. Attach the vertical rudder to the wings by the two 4″ supports. Drill a no. 60 hole in each support ⅛″ in from either end. Peg the support to the cross braces at the upper and lower ends of the rudder. Peg or glue the other end of the supports to the upper surfaces of the wings ¼″ from the back edge and equidistant from the wing tips. With a needle and thread put in the braces or rudder supports as shown.

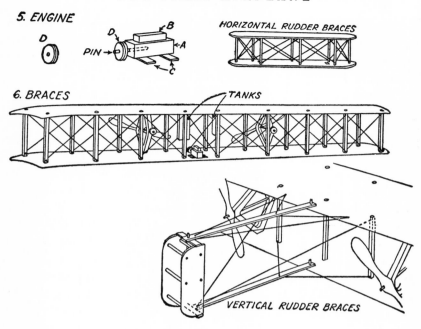

5. ENGINE

D

PIN → D B ←A ←C

HORIZONTAL RUDDER BRACES

6. BRACES

TANKS

VERTICAL RUDDER BRACES

7. Saw out the runners for the sled which was used in place of wheels. Drill no. 45 holes for the struts which should be tapered at both ends to fit into the holes made in the runners and in the crosspieces. Put on the crosspieces. Glue the back braces to the runners and the back struts. Cut the ends at an angle so as to fit against the struts and runners. Peg the 5¾″ braces to the front struts. Set the horizontal rudder on the front ends of the sled. Then peg the braces to the ends of the sled. Make the control lever assembly, and glue or peg it to the brace on the left side of the sled and to the front end of the sled inside of the horizontal rudder. Glue or peg the plane and rudder assembly to the sled. Fasten the braces from the front edge of the upper wing to the sled just back of where it turns upward at the front end.

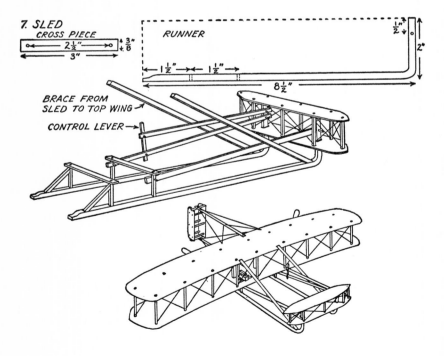

ON EARLY AMERICAN FARMS

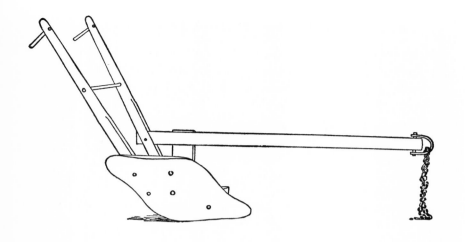

AN EARLY PLOW

THE PLOW in one form or another has been used by man for thousands of years. In colonial America it was still a clumsy wooden tool. Not until about 1800 were any major improvements made in the plow. Thomas Jefferson and Daniel Webster were two of the men who made some changes in it. Later on Charles Newbold and Jethro Wood made plows from iron. With the iron plow it was possible to till the prairie lands whose sod had been too tough for the wooden plow to break, and a whole new section of the country could be cultivated. In a few years the iron plow entirely replaced the wooden one in America.

Materials:

1 pc $\frac{3}{16}$″ x $\frac{1}{4}$″ x 5″—beam
1 pc $\frac{3}{16}$″ x $1\frac{1}{4}$″ x 3″—moldboard
1 pc $\frac{3}{8}$″ x $\frac{1}{2}$″ x $1\frac{1}{4}$″—landside
1 pc $\frac{1}{8}$″ x $\frac{3}{8}$″ x $1\frac{5}{8}$″—brace
1 pc $\frac{1}{8}$″ x $\frac{3}{16}$″ x 4″—left handle
1 pc $\frac{1}{8}$″ x $\frac{3}{16}$″ x $3\frac{3}{4}$″—right handle
1 pc applicator $1\frac{1}{2}$″ long ⎤
1 pc applicator $\frac{3}{4}$″ long   ⎦ braces
2 pc round toothpick $\frac{1}{2}$″ long—hand grips

1. Make a notch $\frac{3}{16}$″ wide and $\frac{1}{8}$″ deep at one end of the beam for the handle to set against the beam. Make an opening $\frac{3}{8}$″ long and $\frac{1}{8}$″ wide $\frac{3}{4}$″ in from the same end of the beam for the upright brace. To make this opening drill three or four no. 45 holes and enlarge with a knife and file. Sandpaper the beam so that it tapers a little at the front end. Make a no. 60 hole down through the beam $\frac{1}{4}$″ from the front end for a clevis and chain.

I. BEAM

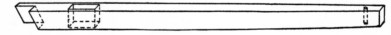

2. Trace the drawing for the moldboard on a piece of $\frac{3}{16}''$ balsa and cut out. With a knife and sandpaper make the moldboard thinner at the shaded points. Drill no. 60 holes as shown at A and B.

3. Make a $\frac{5}{8}''$ x $\frac{1}{8}''$ opening in the landside in the same way as the opening was made in the beam. Cut off the front corner of the landside as shown.

4. Shape the handles and drill no. 45 holes for the cross braces between them. Cut off the lower corner of the left handle so it will fit against the brace when set into place in the opening cut in the landside. Drill no. 52 holes $\frac{1}{4}''$ in from upper end for hand grips.

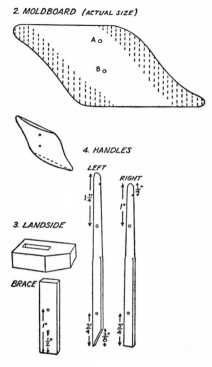

2. MOLDBOARD (ACTUAL SIZE)

4. HANDLES

3. LANDSIDE

BRACE

Set one end of the upright brace into the opening made in the beam and the other end into the opening made in the landside. Peg the brace to the beam and to the landside. Set the lower end of the left handle into the opening in the landside back of the brace. Fasten the right handle to the left handle with the two cross braces. Put the longer brace through the upper holes made in the handles. Set the moldboard against the landside where it was cut off, and glue and peg it to the landside and to the right handle. Put toothpick braces through the holes made in the moldboard and on through holes drilled through the upright brace.

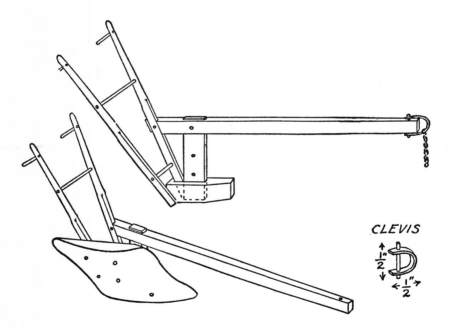

CLEVIS

A WOODEN HARROW

THE OLD triangular harrow was used in colonial days
to get the plowed ground in condition for planting the
seeds. Like his other tools, the harrow was made by the
farmer from wood. He made a framework of heavy sticks
in the shape of an "A" and inserted wooden pegs or teeth
into holes made in this frame. This tool was then dragged
by horses or oxen over the plowed ground to make it ready
for planting.

Materials:

2 small branches or round sticks ⅜″ in diameter and about 6″
    long
1 branch ¼″ in diameter and 4½″ long (or use ¼″ dowels)
17 pc ³⁄₁₆″ x ³⁄₁₆″ x 1½″—pegs or teeth

1. Prepare the two sidepieces as
shown in the diagram. Drill ⅛″
holes for the pegs.

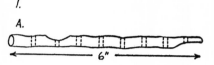

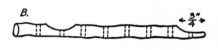

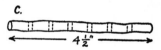

2. Lay piece A on piece B and
insert a peg down through the
holes in A and B. Lay the crosspiece C across the side sections
and in the notches that were cut
or filed out. Peg it fast with toothpick pegs.

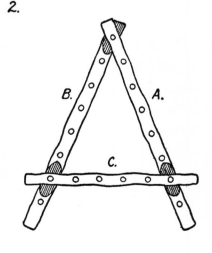

3. Shape the pegs or teeth and insert them in the holes. Each peg should extend below the frame about ¾". Make a set of whipple trees and a clevis and fasten to the front peg with a small chain.

3.

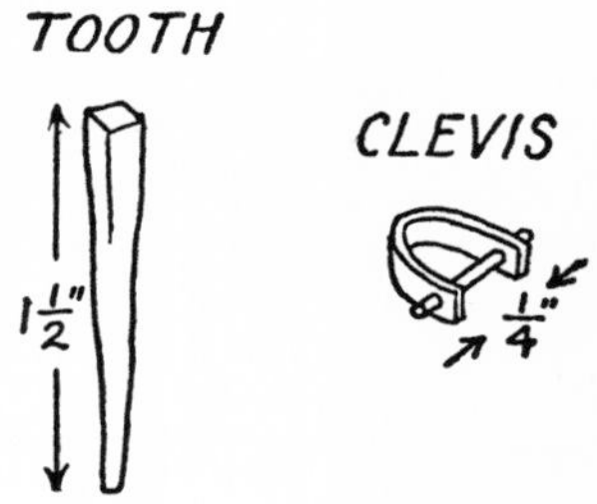

TOOTH

$1\frac{1}{2}$"

CLEVIS

$\frac{1}{4}$"

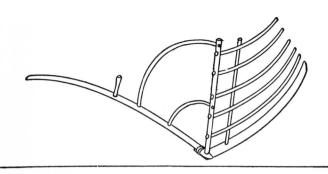

A GRAIN CRADLE

FROM THE BEGINNING of history up to 1831, when Cyrus McCormick invented the reaper, man made only slight changes in his methods of reaping grain. The cradle was the only improvement in the method of grain cutting and was first introduced into this country about the time of the American Revolution, although evidence shows that it was used in Europe some time before that in a more or less crude form.

American ingenuity improved upon the cradle and developed it to its most efficient form. In its earliest form it was a frame of wooden fingers attached to the handle of the scythe. The fingers caught the grain as it was cut so that it could be laid on the ground in good condition, ready for binding into sheaves. In its later form the cradle was made with a heavier blade, shorter handle and fingers which were curved to correspond with the curve of the blade. A man working with an American cradle could cut about two acres of grain in a day.

A GRAIN CRADLE

Materials:

1 pc ⅛" dowel 4½" long—handle
1 pc ⅛" dowel 2" long—frame
1 pc thin metal ¼" x 3"—blade
5 pc no. 1 reed about 3" long—fingers
2 pc no. 1 reed 2" long—brace
1 pc no. 1 reed 3" long—brace
1 round toothpick
(If reed is not available use broom straws.)

1. Soak the 4½" piece of dowel and bend as shown. Drill a no. 60 hole ⅛" from the lower end of the handle. Also drill holes for the two braces and the hand grip.

2. Drill no. 60 holes ⅜" apart for the reed fingers in the 2" piece of dowel. Make the first hole ¼" from one end. Peg the dowel to the handle and put in the braces. Insert one of the fingers in each hole.

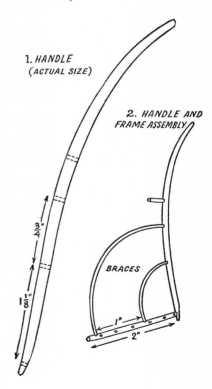

1. HANDLE
(ACTUAL SIZE)

2. HANDLE AND FRAME ASSEMBLY

BRACES

3" 4

1 ⅛"

1"

2"

3. Shape the blade with a file. Cement the blade to the handle. Put a ring of thin metal or wire around the end of the blade and the handle.

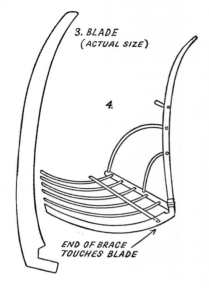

3. BLADE
(ACTUAL SIZE)

4.

END OF BRACE
TOUCHES BLADE

4. Glue a 2″ piece of reed across the fingers, parallel to the upright part of the frame. Have this brace rest on the blade. Insert a ½″ piece of round toothpick in the hole for the hand grip. Bend the fingers to the curve of the blade by holding over a candle flame or after soaking. Cut the fingers off so that the longest one, next to the blade, is 2⅞″, the second one is 2¾″, the third one is 2⅝″, the fourth 2½″, and the last or top finger is 2⅜″ long.

A FLAIL

THRESHING by hand with a flail was the usual method of separating the grain from the straw until a little over one hundred years ago when machines began to replace this slow and laborious operation. A man working with a flail could only thresh out about ten bushels of grain in a day.

The flail, like almost all other farm tools, was made by the farmer himself and consisted of two pieces of wood tied together with a leather thong. The handle was about three and a half feet long and the swiple, or part with which the grain was beaten, was about three feet long. During the long winter months the farmer and his family flailed out the grain on the barn floor.

Materials:

1 pc applicator 5″ long—handle
1 pc ⅛″ x ⅛″ x 3½″—swiple
1 pc of fine thread

Make a shallow groove in the handle ⅛″ from one end with a thin file or knife.

Round off the corners of the swiple with a file or sandpaper and drill a small hole ⅛″ from one end for the thread. Tie the swiple to the handle so that the two pieces are about ¼″ apart.

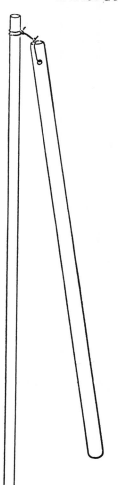

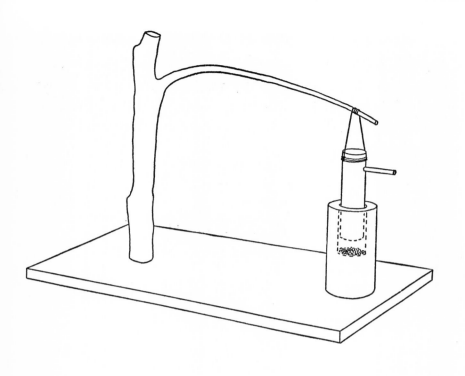

A SAMP MILL

THE SAMP MILL, or the sweep and mortar mill, is an example of the ingenuity of the early American settlers who used it to grind corn. The mortar was made by hollowing out a stump or a section of a tree trunk. A pounding instrument, known as the pestle, made from another block of wood, fitted into the mortar. The pestle, which had a handle on one side, was fastened to the top of a bent sapling or hung from a tree branch. The sapling or branch acted as a spring to pull the pestle up again after it had been pounded down on the corn. This sweep and mortar mill replaced the Indian mortar and pestle which operated entirely by hand. It is said that women used to communicate with their neighbors by pounding on their mortars and also that sailors, caught in a fog, could tell that they were near the shores of Long Island by the sound of the samp mills.

Materials:

1 pc ³⁄₁₆″ x 2½″ x 6″—base
1 pc round stick ¾″ in diameter and 1½″ long—mortar (A piece sawed from a tree branch makes a good mortar.)
1 pc ⅜″ dowel 1½″ long—pestle
1 round toothpick—handle
1 small crotched tree branch about 3½″ long with a branch about 4″ long. Cut from a lilac or similar bush—tree
1 pc thread or string

Drill a ⅜″ hole about ¾″ deep in the center of the mortar and glue the mortar to the base 1″ back from one end.

Drill a small hole in one side of the pestle ⅜″ from the top and insert a ½″ piece of round toothpick for the handle.

Drill a hole in the base about 3″ from the mortar, just large enough for the branch or "tree trunk." Set the tree into the hole. Fasten the pestle to the branch with thread or string so that it hangs over the mortar.

A WATER WHEEL AND
GRIST MILL

WATER, as a source of power, was used by man long
before the first settlers landed on the shores of the New
World. The colonists in North America used water to drive
the great wheels which turned the machinery in the grist
mills and in the saw mills. The colonial farmer took his
grain to the mill which was built beside a small stream
and there it was ground into flour between the heavy, fur-
rowed millstones.

In the middle of the seventeenth century John Winthrop
and his neighbors built a grist mill beside Jordan's Brook

in New London, Connecticut. This picturesque old mill with its gambrel roof and large water wheel is still standing there—a relic of an age now long since gone.

Materials:

2 pc ³⁄₁₆″ x 2¼″ x 2½″—ends
2 pc ¹⁄₁₆″ x 1⅛″ x 4½″—sides
1 pc ¹⁄₁₆″ x 2½″ x 4½″—floor
2 pc ¹⁄₁₆″ x ⅞″ x 4¾″—roof—upper slope
2 pc ¹⁄₁₆″ x 1¹⁄₁₆″ x 4¾″—roof—lower slope
1 pc ¹⁄₁₆″ x 1″ x 1⅜″—door
6 pc ¹⁄₃₂″ x ¹⁄₃₂″ x ¾″—window sash
1 pc 20 gauge wire 3″ long—track
2 pc thin metal ¹⁄₁₆″ x ½″—door hangers
} mill

2 discs ⅛″ thick and 2¼″ in diameter
16 pc ¹⁄₁₆″ x ⅜″ x 1″—blades
1 pc ⅛″ dowel 2¾″ long—shaft
1 pc ³⁄₁₆″ x ½″ x ½″—shaft holder
} wheel

1 pc ⅛″ x ⅝″ x 2½″
2 pc ¹⁄₁₆″ x ⅜″ x 2½″
2 pc ³⁄₃₂″ x ³⁄₃₂″ x 3½″—supports
} mill run

2 pc ¾″ dowel ³⁄₁₆″ long
2 buttonmolds ⅜″ in diameter
} grinders

1 pc ¾″ x 6″ x 9″—A
1 pc ¾″ x 6″ x 6″—B
1 pc ¾″ x 1¼″ x 2½″—C
1 pc ¾″ x 2½″ x 7″—D
} base

1. Saw out the ends. Cut out a 1¼" x ⅞" opening for the door and ½" x ½" openings for windows. The upper edge of each opening should be ¼" from the top edge of the side section. Make lines or grooves with an awl ⅛" apart, lengthwise on each side and end to represent the siding boards. Glue two strips, to represent the window sash, to the inside of each side section across each window opening.

Glue the ends to the bottom board and put on the sides. Glue the roof boards on. Fill in the crack at the peak with plastic wood, or glue a ⅟₁₆" x ⅟₁₆" x 4¾" piece of balsa in the crack and sandpaper it down when dry. Hang the door on a wire track 2½" long. Make the hangers for the door from copper foil or tin ⅟₁₆" wide and ½" long. Make no. 60 holes in the door ⅛" down from the top and ¼" in from each side for the hangers. Put one end of the hanger in the hole and bend the other end so it fits over the track.

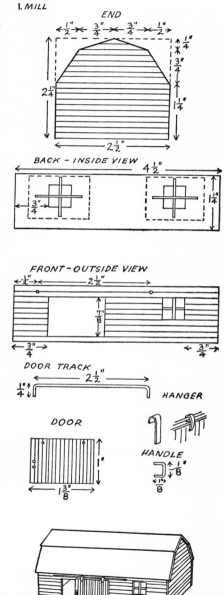

2. Make the grinders by gluing ⅜″ buttonmolds to small checkers or pieces of dowel. Glue them to the floor of the mill.

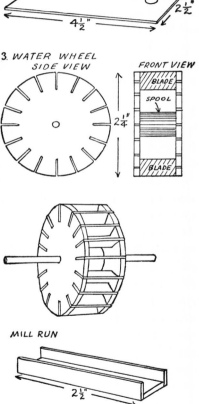

2. GRINDERS

⅜″ BUTTON MOLD

¾″

FLOOR

GRINDERS

4½″

2½″

3. Drill ⅛″ holes through the center of each of the discs to be used for the wheel. Make 16 saw cuts ⅜″ in depth around the circumference of the discs. Saw both discs together so that the cuts correspond with each other. Glue a ¾″ piece cut from a spool between the discs at the center. Be sure to have the saw cuts opposite each other. Insert the blades into the saw cuts. Put the shaft through the holes in the discs and the hole in the spool. The mill run is made by gluing the sidepieces to the bottom piece.

3. WATER WHEEL
SIDE VIEW

FRONT VIEW

BLADE

SPOOL

BLADE

2¼″

MILL RUN

2½″

4. To make the base upon which to mount the mill and the wheel, first make a groove 1½″ in width and ½″ deep 1½″ in from one end of piece A. Make the groove run the full width of the piece. Make saw cuts first and then remove the wood with a chisel. Drill an ⅛″ hole in the center of one end of piece B, ⅛″ down from the top, for the end of the shaft. Then fasten piece B to piece A. Shape piece C as shown and fasten to piece A and B. Then shape piece D and fasten in place. Make a holder in which the end of the shaft can run by filing a groove in a piece ³⁄₁₆″ x ½″ x ½″. Glue the holder to the top of piece D so that the groove will be in line with the hole drilled in piece B for the other end of the shaft. Set the run in the notch cut in C and glue one of the upright supports to each side of the run. Mount the mill on piece B so that the center of the mill is over the end of the shaft.

Stain the model. Use blue paint to represent the water.

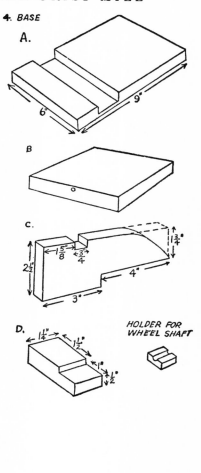

PARTS ASSEMBLED

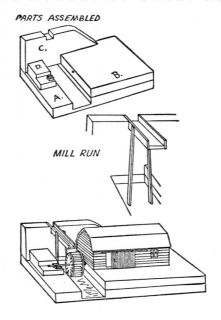

MILL RUN

IN EARLY AMERICAN HOMES

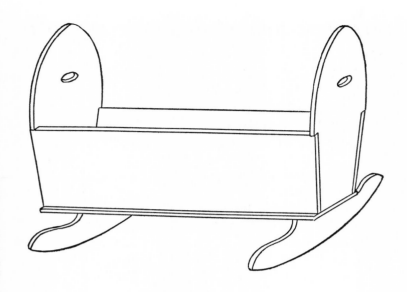

A CRADLE

THE BABIES of colonial America were usually rocked to sleep in a homemade cradle. The cradle is a very ancient piece of furniture and has been in use throughout the world for many centuries. Our colonial forefathers made various types of cradles, some with canopies and some without, some large enough for twins, one in each end, and some big enough for only one small occupant. On the whole, the cradles were simple but sturdily built articles of furniture and many a pioneer baby slept or played in his homemade bed near the great kitchen fireplace while his mother spun thread for his clothing on her spinning wheel.

Materials:

2 pc ¹⁄₁₆″ x 1½″ x 2″—ends
2 pc ¹⁄₁₆″ x 1″ x 3½″—sides
1 pc ¹⁄₁₆″ x 1¼″ x 3½″—bottom
2 pc ¹⁄₁₆″ x ⅝″ x 3″—rockers
1 pc ⅛″ x ⅛″ x 3″—brace

1. Cut out the sides and bottom. *1.*
Trace the drawing for one half
of the end on a piece of tracing
paper. Fold the paper on the dotted line and cut out.

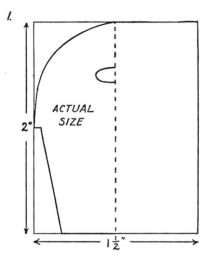

2. To make the ends draw a   *2.*
light line across the center of the
piece from which the end is to
be sawed. Measure in ¹⁄₁₆″ from
each end of this line and make
a dot. Connect this dot with another dot made ¼″ in from each
edge at the bottom of the piece.

Lay the paper pattern on the
board so that the straight edges
of the pattern coincide with the
lines drawn on the wood. Saw

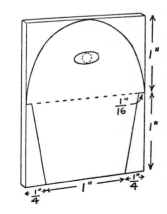

out, then round off the curved edge with fine sandpaper. Drill a no. 43 hole in each end and ½″ from the top. Enlarge hole to correct shape with small round file. Glue the side boards to the endpieces. Glue on the bottom.

3. Make the rockers by tracing the drawing for one half of a rocker on tracing paper. Fold the paper on the dotted line and cut out the pattern. Lay the pattern on the piece of wood so that the straight edge of the pattern coincides with one edge of the board. Draw around the pattern. Saw out, then round off the curved surface of the rocker with sandpaper.

Make a file cut ⅛″ wide and ¹⁄₁₆″ deep in the center of the top edge of each rocker. Shape the brace as shown in the diagram. Set the brace into the openings made in the rockers. Glue or peg this assembly to the bottom of the cradle equidistant from the sides and ends. Stain the model.

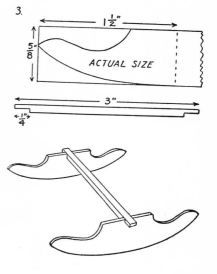

A HORNBOOK

THE HORNBOOK, from which children usually learned their letters, was brought over to this country from England and was used in the elementary schools until after 1700. It consisted of a single sheet of paper about 4″ x 3″ in size mounted on a wooden paddle and covered with a thin sheet of transparent horn. The page always began with a cross to remind the child to say "God spede me ABC" or some other prayer. After that came the alphabet, vowels, some syllables such as ab, eb, ib, da, the Benediction and the Lord's Prayer. Birch bark was often used instead of paper which was very scarce in colonial America. A hole was made in the handle of the paddle through which a string could be tied so that the hornbook could be hung around the child's neck.

Materials:

1 pc ³⁄₁₆″ x 4½″ x 8½″
1 pc paper or thin cardboard 3¾″ x 4¾″
1 pc cellophane, celluloid or other transparent material
    4½″ x 5½″
10 straight pins
    (If birch bark is available it may be used instead of paper.)

Shape the board as shown in the diagram. Stain with an oil stain before putting the paper on the board.

Draw a design for a border similar to the one shown. Print the alphabet, vowels, Benediction and the Lord's Prayer on the paper. Paste the paper on the board and cover with the transparent material which should be fastened on with short pieces cut from the head end of pins, or tiny tacks, nails or escutcheon pins.

If the birch bark is used fasten it to a board with thumb tacks until dry before lettering it. Do not cover the bark with transparent material.

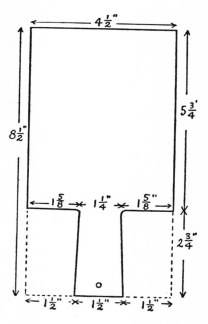

I. *BOARD*

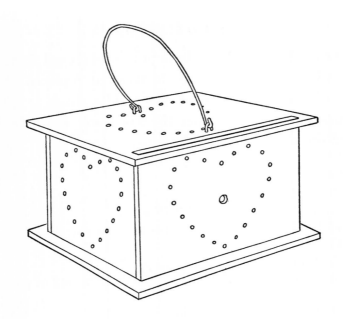

A FOOT STOVE

IN COLONIAL DAYS in America women and children
carried foot stoves to church with them, because the un-
heated churches were cold and damp, and the sermons
were long. These little stoves were wooden boxes or wooden
frames, with a metal box or can inside to hold hot coals.
Holes, usually in the form of circles or hearts, were made
in the sides, ends and top of the box to allow the heat
from the coals to escape.

Materials:
1 pc ⅛″ x 2⅛″ x 3″—front
1 pc ⅛″ x 2″ x 3″—back
2 pc ⅛″ x 2″ x 2¼″—ends
2 pc ⅛″ x 3″ x 3½″—top and bottom
1 pc 20 gauge wire 5″ long

A FOOT STOVE

1. Saw out the parts as listed. Make a pattern of a heart and use it to draw the outline of a heart on the front piece. Place the pattern equidistant from the edges. Mark the holes as shown and drill holes about ⅟₁₆″ in diameter. These holes were to allow the heat to escape. Also drill an ⅛″ hole in the center of this piece.

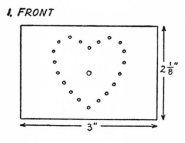

1. FRONT

Use the heart outlined on front piece as pattern to make hearts on the back, top and ends. Do not make the hole in the center of these pieces, however. Lay the front section on the other pieces so that the heart will be equidistant from the sides in each case. Mark through the holes with an awl to make the outline of the heart. Drill ⅟₁₆″ holes.

2. Make an opening 3″ long and ⅛″ wide in the top section ¼″ in from the front edge and ¼″ in from each end. The front piece will slide up and down through this opening.

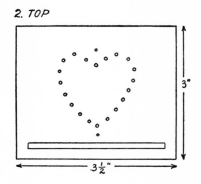

2. TOP

3. Drill two small holes for the hooks or screw eyes which will hold the wire handle. Make the handle and fasten it to the top with tiny screw eyes or wire hooks. Shape the handle by bending it around a can about 2″ in diameter.

4. Glue the back to the ends. Glue the bottom and the top to the ends and back. The top and bottom will extend ¼″ all around. When putting the top on, insert the front into the opening in the top so that it will slide up and down and will thus determine the exact position of the top. Set a metal can or bottle top about 1½″ in diameter inside the stove to hold the coals.

3. HANDLE

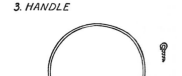

4. FRONT VIEW

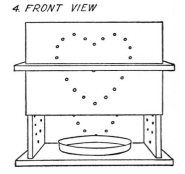

A SETTLE

ALONGSIDE the great fireplaces in the kitchens of colonial America usually stood the settle, a simply constructed piece of furniture, but very well adapted for use in those days. It had a high back and a seat, the front of which went all the way down to the floor. The settle, thus constructed, kept the cold drafts out and the heat from the fireplace in. Some settles were made with a chest beneath the seat for the storage of whatever articles the housewife wished to keep there.

Materials:

2 pc ¹⁄₁₆″ x 1″ x 3½″—ends
1 pc ¹⁄₁₆″ x 1″ x 2½″—front
2 pc ¹⁄₁₆″ x 1″ x 2⅜″—seat and bottom
4 pc ¹⁄₁₆″ x ⅛″ x ⅞″—seat and bottom supports
1 pc ¹⁄₁₆″ x ½″ x 2½″—top
1 pc ¹⁄₁₆″ x 2½″ x 3½″—back

1. Saw out the end sections as shown in the diagram. Saw on dotted lines. Glue the seat and bottom supports to the inside of the end sections. The bottom support is ⅛″ from the lower end and the support for the seat is ⅞″ from the same end. Glue the bottom board in place between the ends. Put on the front piece.

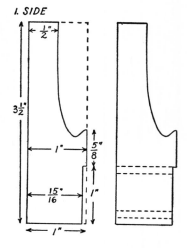

I. SIDE

2. Cut the seat board lengthwise into two pieces—one ¾″ wide and one piece ¼″ wide. Glue the ¼″ piece in place. The front part of the seat is just set in place and can be removed, as the lower part of the settle was often used as a chest for storage.

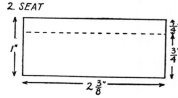

2. SEAT

3. Notch out the top piece as shown and glue in place.

4. Cut the back section lengthwise into four parts each ⅝″ x 3½″. Apply glue to the back edges of the top, the end sections and the bottom. Fit the back boards in place.

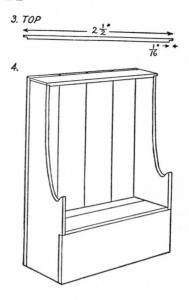

3. *TOP*

4.

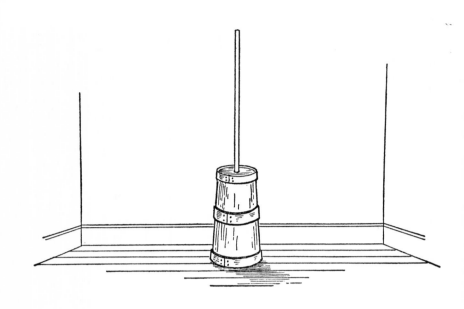

A BUTTER CHURN

IN THE CORNER of many a colonial kitchen stood a
wooden churn with a long handle, on the lower end of
which was a wooden dasher. The making of butter was
one of the duties of the women and girls of the eighteenth
century and many an hour was spent moving the dasher
up and down in the cream until butter was formed. Then
cold water was poured into the churn, the dasher was
turned and the butter was thus "gathered" and removed
from the churn, leaving buttermilk behind. The butter was
then worked in the wooden butter bowl and pressed into
butter molds, after which it was ready for eating.

A BUTTER CHURN

Materials:

1 pc dowel or round stick 1¼" in diameter and 2¼" long—barrel
or churn (A piece of broom handle or window shade roller
may be used, or the barrel may be shaped from a piece of
balsa. The dimensions given make a good model although it
can be larger or smaller.)

1 pc applicator 4¼" long ⎤
2 pc ¹⁄₁₆" x ³⁄₃₂" x ¾"   ⎬ dasher
                            ⎦
3 pc ¹⁄₃₂" x ¼" x 4"—bands around churn
1 disc ¹⁄₁₆" thick and 1" in diameter—cover

Drill a ¾″ hole down through the center of the round stick or dowel to within ¼″ of the bottom or 2″ deep. With a knife, file, and sandpaper, shape the barrel as shown in the diagram. It should be about 1″ in diameter at the top and 1¼″ at the bottom. Soak the bands of balsa and put them around the churn one at the top, one at the bottom, and one in the middle. Allow the top band to extend ⅛″ above the top of the barrel and so form a place for the cover. Hold the bands in place with rubber bands until dry, then cement the ends together. Again use the rubber bands until the cement sets.

Drill a no. 43 hole in the center of the cover. Drill no. 45 holes in the center of the dasher paddles. Glue these pieces to the handle so as to make a cross. Put the dasher into the barrel and put on the cover.

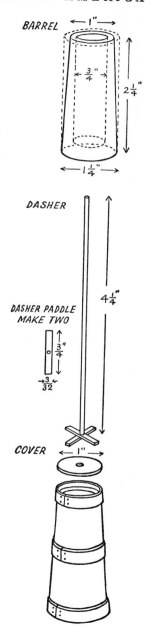

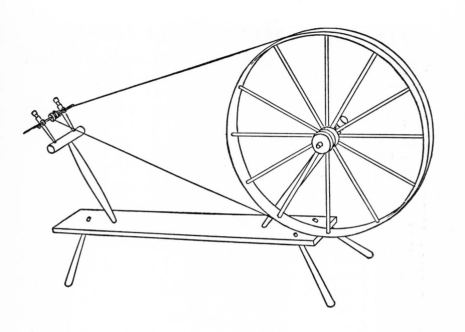

A WOOL WHEEL

THE WHIRR of the wool wheel was a familiar sound
in the homes of early America. The women and girls spun
all the yarn which was later made into clothing for the
entire family. The wool wheel, also called the great wheel,
replaced the distaff and hand spindle and was a far more
efficient means of spinning. The spinner stood beside the
large wheel and made it rotate by striking the spokes with
a wooden stick. A cord or belt connected the large wheel
with a pulley on the spindle, which was mounted on a post
at the other end of the spinning wheel. When the wheel
was rotated by the spinner the spindle, on which the yarn
was wound, revolved very rapidly. Spinning wheels were

in use in most homes in America until about a hundred years ago and can still be found in many an attic.

Materials:

1 pc ³⁄₁₆″ x ¾″ x 6″—base
2 pc ⅛″ dowel 1½″ long—back leg
1 pc ⅛″ dowel 2″ long—front leg
1 embroidery hoop about 5″ in diameter—large wheel
1 pc ⅜″ dowel ¾″ long—hub
1 pc applicator 1¼″ long—axle
16 pc applicator 2¼″ long—spokes
1 pc ¼″ dowel 4″ long—wheel post
1 pc ¼″ dowel 3″ long—spindle post
1 pc ¼″ dowel 1½″ long—spindle holder
1 pc ⅛″ dowel ¼″ long—pulley
2 pc ⅛″ dowel 1¼″ long—upright posts
1 pin or wire 2″ long—spindle (Hat pin or corsage pin may be used.)
2 pc leather about ¹⁄₃₂″ x ¹⁄₁₆″ x 1″

1. Shape the wheel post and the spindle post as shown. Taper the lower ends to about ⅛″ in diameter. Drill a no. 45 hole ½″ down from the top of the wheel post. Make the groove in the wheel post with a file. The groove is ¼″ down from the top. Make spindle post and 3 legs as shown in diagrams.

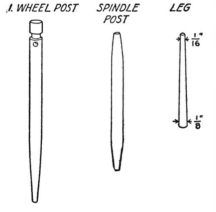

I. WHEEL POST   SPINDLE POST   LEG

2. Drill ³⁄₁₆″ holes in the base at X and Y for the posts, and no. 43 holes at A, B, C, for the legs. Drill the holes so that the legs and posts will set into the base at an angle. The hole for the wheel post at Y is off center and should be ½″ in from the front edge of the base, and 1¾″ from the end. The hole for the spindle post at X is in the center of the base and 1¼″ in from the other end. Set the posts and legs in the holes.

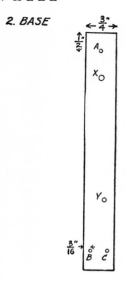

2. BASE

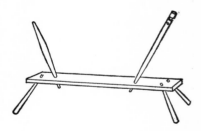

3. Make the wheel. Shape the hub as shown. Make the groove with a small round file before sawing the ¾" piece off. Drill a no. 43 hole through the center of the hub. Drill a no. 60 hole ⅛" in from one end of the axle. Insert the other end of the axle into the hole in the wheel post. Put the wheel on the axle and put a peg in the hole in the axle to hold it on.

4. Drill no. 43 holes ¼" in from each end of the spindle support for the two upright posts which are shaped from 1¼" pieces of ⅛" dowel. Also drill an ⅛" hole in the spindle support equidistant from each end. Drill no. 45 holes ⅜" down from the top of these two posts for the leather loops in which the spindle will turn. Insert the posts into the holes made in the spindle support.

Make the pulley from a ¼" piece of ⅛" dowel through which a pinhole has been drilled lengthwise. Put the pulley on the spindle and fasten the spindle to the posts with loops made from very thin leather or black paper or cloth. Set the spindle assembly on the spindle post. Run a thread or string around the pulley and the large wheel.

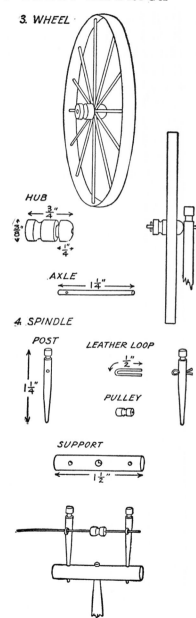

3. WHEEL

HUB

¾"

¾"

¼"

AXLE

1¼"

4. SPINDLE

POST

1¼"

LEATHER LOOP

½"

PULLEY

SUPPORT

1½"

IN EARLY AMERICAN VILLAGES

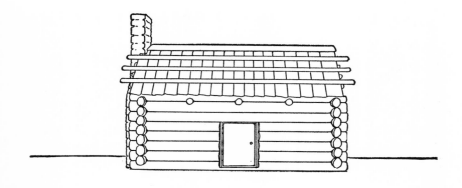

A LOG CABIN

THE LOG CABIN is a true symbol of early America. These sturdy dwellings, usually built by community effort, were the first homes of the pioneers. The logs were notched at each end and were laid one on another so as to interlock at the ends. A roof or wooden slabs usually covered the cabin. Mud and sticks were used to fill in the cracks between the logs. The chimney was often made from small logs plastered with mud.

Materials:

16 pc ⅜" dowel 7" long—sides
14 pc ⅜" dowel 5" long—ends
2 pc ⅜" dowel 3⅝" long ⎤
2 pc ⅜" dowel 2¾" long ⎟ gable ends
2 pc ⅜" dowel 2" long ⎟
2 pc ⅜" dowel 1¼" long ⎦
7 pc ¼" dowel 7" long—roof rafters
3 pc ¼" dowel 5" long—crossbeams
28 pc ¹⁄₃₂" x ¾" x 3"—roof slabs
1 pc ¹⁄₃₂" x ½" x 7"—ridge board

6 pc ⅛″ dowel 7¼″ long—roof slab binders

1 pc soft wood ¾″ x 2½″ x 6″—chimney (Or ¼″ and ⅛″ dowel
  if chimney is made from logs)

2 pc ¹⁄₁₆″ x ⅜″ x 1¾″—doorframe

1 pc ⅛″ x 1⅛″ x 1¾″—door

2 pc leather ¹⁄₁₆″ x ³⁄₁₆″ x ½″—hinges

1. File a notch with a round file ½″ in from each end of two of the 7″ logs, or make a notch with a knife. Make the notches about ⅛″ deep and about ⅜″ long.

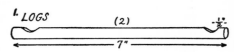

2. Then file similar notches in all of the 5″ logs and in twelve of the 7″ logs. Make, however, one notch on the upper side and one on the lower side of each of these logs. Lay the two 7″ logs, with one notch in them, on the workbench with the notch upward, and lay two of the 5″ logs across them so that the lower notch of the shorter log fits into the notch cut in the longer log. Peg or glue together to make a firm foundation. Continue in this way until the cabin is five logs high. Saw out openings for the door and the window. The door opening should be 1¼″ x 1¾″ or down through four logs and part way through the lower log. Make

the window opening about ¾″ wide and down through two logs. Then continue laying the logs until the cabin is 7 logs high. Finish the sides of the cabin by making notches in the remaining two 7″ logs as shown. Make notches ½″ from the ends in one side of each of the three ¼″ dowels being used for crossbeams. Lay these crossbeams across the upper side logs so as to bind them together. Lay the last two 7″ logs on top of these crossbeams and the top end logs. Build the gable ends up from the short sections of logs which become shorter and shorter as the peak of the gable is approached. Glue or peg the logs which form the gable end together as they are laid one upon the other. Make one notch at each end of the roof rafters and set them over the logs which form the gable ends. If the topmost roof rafter is not quite high enough to give a gradual slope to the roof, glue a ½″ piece of ¼″ dowel to the last log of the gable end. Then lay the last rafter over these two pieces.

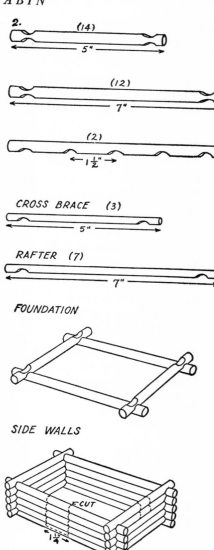

2.

(14)

5″

(12)

7″

(2)

1½″

CROSS BRACE   (3)

5″

RAFTER   (7)

7″

FOUNDATION

SIDE WALLS

CUT

1¾

3. Shape the chimney as shown. Make grooves with a knife or saw to represent logs. If small logs are to be used, build up the chimney in the same way as the cabin was built.

Cover the roof with slabs, which should overlap each other by about ¼". Glue them on and also glue or peg the pieces of ⅛" dowel lengthwise on the roof, three on each side. Soak the ¹⁄₃₂" x ½" x 7" pieces of balsa and bend it around a ⅜" dowel. When dry glue it to the peak of the roof to cover the opening where the slabs meet.

Glue the two sides of the doorframe in place. Drill a no. 60 hole in the door for the latch-string and hang the door on the leather hinges. Cover the window with oiled paper.

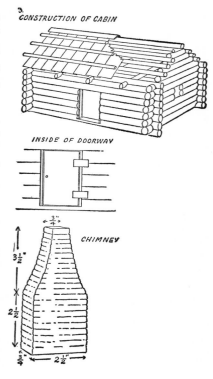

CONSTRUCTION OF CABIN

INSIDE OF DOORWAY

CHIMNEY

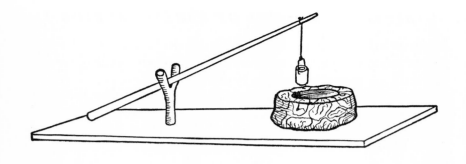

A WELL SWEEP

IN COLONIAL TIMES wells supplied water for the household and a well sweep was used to raise the water from the well. It consisted of a long pole and a post or crotched stick. The post or crotched stick was set in the ground near the well and the pole was laid in the crotch or pivoted to the post with a wooden peg. A bucket was fastened to the small end of the pole by a rope, and could thus be lowered empty into the water and raised brimful. It was a simple device and may still be seen occasionally today.

Materials:
1 pc ⅛″ x 3″ x 6″—base
1 pc ⅜″ x ⅜″ x 2″—post (Or use crotched stick 2″ long)
1 pc ⅛″ dowel or thin branch about 6″ long—pole
1 block about ¼″ x ⅜″ x 1″—weight
4 pc ¹⁄₁₆″ x ¾″ x 1½″ ⎤
4 pc ⅛″ x ⅛″ x 1″ ⎦ frame around well
1 pc ⅜″ dowel ⅜″ long—bucket
1 pc 20 gauge wire 1¼″ long—bail

Make a hole 1″ square in the base ½″ from one end. Make a bottomless box, set it over this opening and glue it to the base. Glue the 1″ posts in the corners of this box.

Notch out the post as shown in the diagram. Taper the piece of dowel so that one end is smaller. Drill a no. 60 hole 1½″ from the thickest end of the pole. Drill another hole ⅜″ down from the top of the post. Glue the post to the base 1½″ from one end, and equidistant from the sides. Fasten the pole to the post with a toothpick peg allowing toothpick to protrude on either side. Glue the weight to the thickest end of the pole.

Drill out the inside of the ⅜″ piece of dowel to a depth of ¼″ for the bucket. Make pinholes for the bail. Attach the bucket to the pole with thread.

If the crotched stick is used drill a hole in the base for it. The wall or frame around the well can be made from small stones, using plaster of Paris, claystone or a flour and sand mixture for mortar. See diagram.

Make a box about two inches high and set the well sweep assembly on top of the box like a cover. Set a small tin can inside the box beneath the opening and fill it with water.

A WELL SWEEP

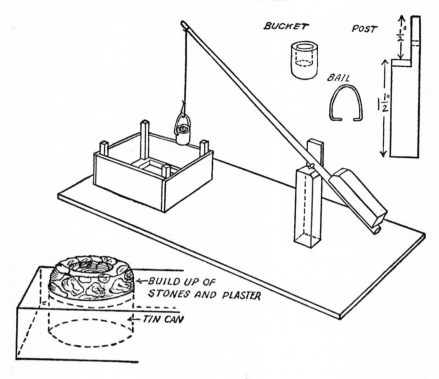

BUCKET

POST

BAIL

←BUILD UP OF
STONES AND PLASTER

TIN CAN

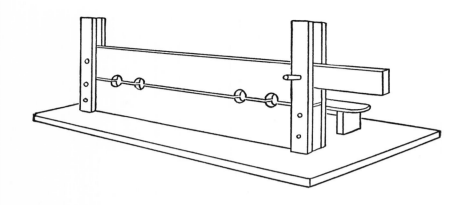

THE STOCKS

EVERY colonial New England community built stocks, an instrument for the punishment of wrongdoers which can be traced back to the twelfth century. The stocks were made from two timbers, the upper one of which could be raised and lowered. Holes were made for the legs of the culprit and in some cases holes were also made for the arms. The victim sat on a low bench placed behind the stocks, placed his legs and arms in the holes and was then locked in.

Our colonial forefathers punished those who had done wrong in a harsh and direct way. The punishment was usually public and was meant to be an example to others as well as a punishment for the one who had broken the laws of the day, so the stocks were placed on the village green. They were generally used for men but women were sometimes made to sit in them also. Men were locked in the stocks for such offenses as stealing, breaking the Sabbath, or gambling. While so confined they made excellent targets for the ridicule of passers-by.

Materials:

1 pc ³⁄₁₆″ x 3″ x 6″—base
1 pc ³⁄₁₆″ x 1½″ x 6″—horizontal section
4 pc ⅛″ x ¼″ x 2″—uprights
2 pc ³⁄₁₆″ x ½″ x ⅝″—bench supports
1 pc ⅛″ x ½″ x 5″—bench seat
2 pc applicator ¾″ long—pegs

1. Saw out the horizontal board. Drill 2 pairs of ¼″ holes ¾″ apart. Saw the board into two parts. Round off the corner of the upper part.

2. Glue or peg the uprights to the lower section as shown in the drawing.

3. Set the upper section in place and drill no. 45 holes through the two uprights and the upper section. Put the applicator pegs in these holes.

4. Glue the assembly to the base. Make bench for the victim to sit on and glue it to the base.

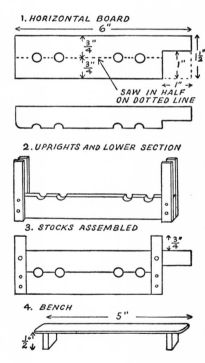

1. HORIZONTAL BOARD

SAW IN HALF ON DOTTED LINE

2. UPRIGHTS AND LOWER SECTION

3. STOCKS ASSEMBLED

4. BENCH

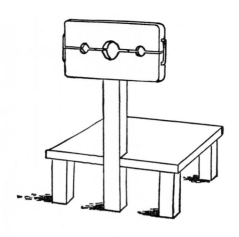

THE PILLORY

THE PILLORY, sometimes known as the stretch-neck, was to be seen in a prominent place in most colonial villages. There were several variations of the pillory but in general it consisted of an upright board, made in two sections, with holes which fitted round the offender's neck and wrists. The board was mounted on a post and a platform was built on which the victim stood. It was used in England for hundreds of years and was transplanted to America by the English colonists. Even as late as 1803, records show that this instrument of punishment was used in Boston. Men and women were pilloried for numerous reasons, among which were arson, lying, fortune-telling, witchcraft, drunkenness, forgery, dishonesty. The pillory was usually placed in the public square or the churchyard and the pilloried prisoners were often targets for stones and snowballs.

THE PILLORY

Materials:

1 pc $\frac{3}{16}''$ x 2'' x $2\frac{1}{2}''$—platform
4 pc $\frac{1}{4}''$ x $\frac{3}{8}''$ x 1''—legs
1 pc $\frac{1}{4}''$ x $\frac{3}{8}''$ x $2\frac{3}{4}''$—upright post
1 pc $\frac{3}{16}''$ x $1\frac{1}{4}''$ x 2''—headboard
2 pc 18 gauge wire 1'' long
2 straight pins

1. Saw out opening in the platform for the upright post. Glue the legs to the corners of the platform $\frac{1}{8}''$ in from each edge.

2. Cut a notch $\frac{3}{16}''$ deep and $\frac{1}{4}''$ long in one end of the post for the headboard.

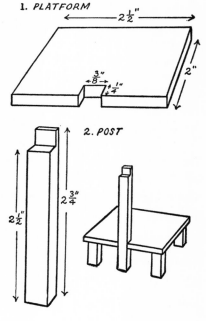

1. PLATFORM

2. POST

3. Make a ⅜" hole in the center of the headboard and an ⅛" hole ⅜" in from each end. Cut the board lengthwise through the center of the three holes. Insert pins into the lower part of the board on either side of the hole for the victim's neck. Cut off the heads of the pins. Drill no. 60 holes in the upper section directly above the pins to a depth of ¼". Set the lower part of the headboard in the notch made in the upper end of the post and glue or peg fast. Set the upper part of the headboard on the lower part.

Make wire staples and insert into pinholes made in the ends of the headboard to lock the sections together when victim is in pillory.

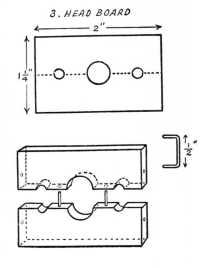

3. HEAD BOARD

THE DUCKING STOOL

THE DUCKING STOOL, once popular in England and America, was most often used to punish women gossips, although women were sometimes ducked for other offenses. Men, too, were forced to sit in the chair and endure a plunge into cold water for talking too much about their neighbors, or for making bad bread or for brewing bad beer. Married couples who could not get along together were sometimes tied back to back and submerged together in the water.

There were several variations of the ducking stool, but they all served the same purpose. The most common one was known as the trebucket and consisted of a long beam set on a post near the water. It was so made that it could be swung around by hand parallel to the water's edge by means of a simple pivotal device while the victim was being tied fast in the chair. When the device was not in use it was fastened to a post so that mischievous children could not duck each other.

Materials:

1 pc $\frac{3}{16}''$ x $2\frac{1}{2}''$ x 6"—base
1 pc $\frac{3}{16}''$ x $\frac{1}{4}''$ x 9"—lever
1 pc $\frac{1}{4}''$ x $\frac{3}{8}''$ x $1\frac{1}{4}''$—upright post
1 pc $\frac{1}{4}''$ dowel 1" long—post to which beam can be locked
1 pc $\frac{1}{8}''$ x 1" x 1"—back ⎤
1 pc $\frac{1}{8}''$ x $\frac{3}{4}''$ x 1"—bottom ⎬ chair
2 pc $\frac{1}{8}''$ x $\frac{3}{8}''$ x $\frac{3}{4}''$—sides ⎦
2 toothpicks

THE DUCKING STOOL

1. Saw out parts as described. Make a notch with a file in one end of the upright post. Make the notch about ¼" in width, or just wide enough so that the long lever will fit easily into it, and ⅜" deep. Drill a no. 60 hole ⅛" down from the top of the post. Drill another no. 60 hole down through the bottom of the notch lengthwise of the post. Measure down ½" from the top and saw the notched end off. Put a toothpick peg or pin into the hole made through the notched section and the post, thus holding the two pieces together so that the upper section will turn or pivot. Glue or peg this assembly to the base 1" from one end and equidistant from the sides.

Drill a no. 60 hole about 1" (B) from one end of the long lever, and another hole 5" from the same end (A).

2. Cut out the parts for the chair as shown in the diagram. Assemble the chair by gluing the parts together. Glue the chair to the end of the lever. Set the lever into the notch made in the post so that hole A will coincide with the holes in the sides of the notched section of the post. Put a toothpick peg or pin through these holes allowing the beam to see-saw on it.

3. Drill a ¼" hole ¾" from the rear end of the base and about ¼" off center. Insert the 1" piece of dowel. Drill a hole in this dowel so that a toothpick can be put through hole B in the beam and into this hole, thus holding the lever in position when not in use. To lock the lever to the post wrap a piece of fine chain around it and the post and make a tiny padlock from a thin piece of ¼" dowel or cork and a piece of wire.

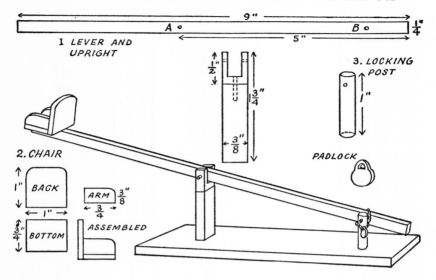

1 LEVER AND UPRIGHT

3. LOCKING POST

2. CHAIR

BACK 1"

ARM 3/8"

BOTTOM

ASSEMBLED

PADLOCK